Sister Wendy Contemplates...
THE ICONIC JESUS

This book
is dedicated to my dear friend Gina Rozner
who has worked so hard to make my books known,
and to all the Sisters in the Monastery who helped me
with pictures, especially Sister Lesley
and Sister Veronica.

SISTER WENDY BECKETT

Sister Wendy Contemplates...

The Iconic Jesus

ST PAULS

Cover design: C. González, ssp.
Reprographics: DX Imaging, Watford, Herts,UK
Cover illustration: *Christ at the Well*, Aidan Hart

Published by ST PAULS, UK
Copyright © ST PAULS, UK 2011

ISBN: 978-0-85439-812-6

Set by C. González, ssp.
Printed by Gutenberg Press, Malta

ST PAULS is an activity of the priests and brothers of the Society of St Paul
who proclaim the Gospel through the media of social communication.

Contents

The Blessing of Christ Our Saviour — 161

Introduction

T here are countless paintings of Our Lord Jesus Christ: on canvas, on board, on walls, on glass. There are countless statues too, from a tiny ivory Jesus in the British Museum to the huge Christ of Rio de Janeiro holding His hands in blessing over the harbour. Almost every Old Master has portrayed Him, and some of these works are great masterpieces. We think of Michelangelo's heroic Christ at the Last Judgement, or Leonardo's Christ at the Last Supper, Rembrandt's poignant images of a Jewish Jesus, or El Greco's flame-like Christ, all passion and energy. In all of these I have taken delight for many years. Yet, when I come to think of it, my delight is often more in the art itself than in what the painting reveals of Jesus. After all, nobody knows what he looked like, so what we are seeing is what Titian imagined Jesus looked like, or Rubens or Bellini. These are interesting men and their imagined Jesus is interesting too. But I do not want to pray to an imagined Jesus. Looking at these lovely images can, at best, urge me to turn away and look within.

It is altogether different when we turn from Western art to the iconic art of the Eastern Church. The western artist is expressing his personality in what he paints, he draws on his inventive powers, his style is unique to himself. But the icon is hardly art at all on those terms. The iconographer was morally prohibited from invention, and it would have been regarded as the gravest of infidelities if he were to attempt to show his personality. When a great genius like Rublev devotes himself to icon painting, his work cannot but be different because of his genius, but this is incidentally: it is in no way willed or desired. Icon painting is a form of prayer. One was called to it as to a priestly vocation. There were rules, not only regulating what was to be painted and how, but the way the painter was to live. He was to conduct his life with the seriousness of one called to glorify God, prayerful and abstinent, seeking only God's glory and never his own. If we look at the face of Jesus in the icons, he is never showing 'personality'. How Jesus looked was established, the Church considered, by the Mandylion, that image not made by human hands but imprinted by Jesus Himself on a cloth held out to Him. This may have been legend but it established the course on which icon painting was to travel. What was painted was not invented, but true. The image of Jesus, or, for that matter, of Mary and the Saints, never shows any 'emotion', in the psychological sense. This is integral to the eternal truth in which Jesus lives. Certainly there are shades of difference between the various iconic Christs, but there is no instance say, of a smiling Christ or of a displeased Christ. He is always Jesus Christ, always the same through all ages.

These selfless images that we call icons have one function only, to put us in touch with the world of grace. We are taken out of our own world as we contemplate, and drawn into this holy world, where God is free to love us as He desires. Contemplating an icon is a serious business. We need to devote time to it, and to be still and silent. I am almost abashed to be offering you so many images at one time. If we just leaf through the book, we will miss its potential to change what we are into what God would have us be, that infinitely free and joyful creature. What I have written about each of these icons of Jesus is painfully inadequate, but I console myself that you do not really need it. It is not in words that we respond to the icon, but at a level far deeper and more immediate. Obviously, I cannot tell you how to use this book, but I will pray for all who use it, hoping that the Iconic Jesus will bless them and draw them to Himself.

1.
The Icon
of the Virgin and Child

6th or 7th century,
Temple Gallery, London.

1. THE ICON OF THE VIRGIN AND CHILD
6th or 7th century

1. The Icon of the Virgin and Child

6th or 7th century

T his is one of the earliest images of Christ, perhaps the very earliest, and it is also the most moving. In the centuries to come, there will be countless attempts to depict Jesus, both in the East and in the West. Yet, not even the greatest of artists has created an image that I find equal to this in power. This is Jesus, literally, at the beginning. He is held in a gleaming mandorla, which recalls Mary's womb. It is both abstract – a concept to indicate the holiness of this Child – and yet, seemingly, material, in that Mary clasps it with a tenacious grip. In fact, the intensity of her involvement is shown by that clenched hand: her face looks away from us, abstracting from the scene, so that all of our attention will be fixed on the little Jesus. He is a divine Child, like no other in art. There is no attempt here to show us a beautiful baby. This Child has rough, red curls, intense dark eyes, a long straight nose (very like His mother's) and is robed in purple and white, suggestive of His imperial dignity. One small hand, seemingly outstretched in blessing, is dwarfed by the clenched fist of His mother which forms a background. The other may be holding a roll of parchment, but the icon is too old for these details still to be clear. What makes the image unforgettable, is the expression on the Child's face. This is not, by any means, that serene and all-powerful Jesus with whom we are familiar. This is a tense Child, very well aware of the complexities of being human. Those dark eyes, that straight, strong mouth, that pale face, do not summon us to rest content in the answers. No, they summon us to join with Jesus in seeking the answers. He calls us to partnership, to enter with Him into the immense responsibility of being human. Jesus came so that we might receive the love of God, and in this love become what we were created to become, full and beautiful human creatures. This is not a cosy message, it offers no conventional comfort. We might call it a challenge, and yet, as this icon makes so poignantly clear, it is a challenge that Jesus, fully man, enters into with us. This is not a God who looks down on our struggles, graciously providing the help that we need. This is a God who, right from the start, symbolically in His mother's womb, bares all the problems and the struggles and the difficulties with us. He will save us, even if it kills Him, and as Mary knows, and as we know, it will indeed kill Him.

The little figure is not quite in proportion: the head, that most moving head, is too large for the small cramped body. It is as if Jesus is telling us that he has come into our world and yet will not fit into it. Man though He is, He supersedes our understanding and our values. Yet, man that he is, this loneliness will pain Him. It is a loneliness that all His followers will come to share. "My kingdom is not of this world". He tells us that we too are not of this world. "If you were of this world, the world would love you as its own... you do not belong to the world... I chose you out of the world". He chose us to search with Him, in Him, and because of Him.

14

2.
The Finding
in the Temple

Late 15th century, Novgorod,
Temple Gallery, London.

2. THE FINDING IN THE TEMPLE
Late 15th century

2 . The Finding in the Temple

Late 15th century

We know of only one incident in the early life of Jesus. When He was twelve, His parents took Him to Jerusalem for the Passover. When they were travelling home at the end of the feast, each thinking the Child was with the other, or among their relatives and acquaintances, they found that He was missing. They returned in great distress to look for Him. This is every parent's nightmare, losing a child and, of course, in this case the anguish was even greater. God had entrusted His Son to them, and they had failed His trust. After three days He was found "in the Temple, sitting in the midst of the doctors, listening to them and asking them questions". It was a traumatic moment for both parents and Child. Mary felt forced to rebuke Him: "Son why have you done this to us? Did you not know that your father and I have been searching for You in sorrow?" Any parent would see this unexplained absence as an act of thoughtless cruelty. How could He 'not know' what His mysterious absence meant to them? But the twelve-year-old Jesus is equally astonished. "Why did you search for Me? Did you not know that I had to be in my Father's House?" St Luke remarks sadly "they did not understand what He said to them".

It is a crucial moment in adolescence when we realise that those closest to us 'do not understand'. It seemed obvious to Jesus that the Temple, where His Father was so loved and glorified, was His natural place, His home even. Being taken to Jerusalem for the Passover had meant for Him a fulfilment and a joy that He had taken for granted needed no explanation. The icon shows a Mary and Joseph motionless to one side, huddled together, exhausted and grieving. For all His closeness to His family, there seems an infinite distance between the weary husband and wife and the radiant Child sitting with the doctors of the Law. They are not receptive doctors, we can see one actually turning away, and one would long to hear the dialogue between them. Perhaps the Child was experiencing a second disillusionment. What wisdom was He finding here in His Father's house? Whatever questions were asked and answered (or not answered) this was the first opportunity that Jesus had to enter into the heart of the religious life of His people. It ended in sorrow, sorrow for having wounded His beloved parents and sorrow at His own lack of understanding of how things worked. It casts a strange and unique light upon the difficulties of His growing up. Scripture tells us that He came back to Nazareth with His parents and set Himself to obey them: "He was subject to them". Obedience was to become an overriding principle in His life. It was obedience to His Father. He was to tell His disciples that He did not act "of His own accord": He looked to His Father and obeyed. "I solemnly assure you, that the Son cannot do anything by Himself – He can only do what He sees the Father doing. For whatever the Father does the Son does likewise". This absolute surrender to His Father, which governed the life of Jesus and would lead Him to His sacrificial death, began at Nazareth, where He understood the need to obey His parents.

3.
Jesus Amidst the Doctors of the Law

Early 16th century, Novgorod,
The Menil Collection,
Houston.

3. JESUS AMIDST THE DOCTORS OF THE LAW
Early 16th century

3. Jesus Amidst the Doctors of the Law
Early 16th century

This wonderful icon shows the young Jesus in the full flow of His happiness at being within 'His Father's House'. As yet, His parents have not found Him, and He is blissfully unaware that they are searching the city, distraught with the most terrible anxiety. The icon painter shows us a beautiful young prince, dominating the interior of the Temple, His whole heart set upon "listening to the doctors and asking them questions". One cannot feel that the answers that He received would have satisfied a mind and a heart that was so intimately united to the Father. It was from this Temple that His antagonists would later arise. They would break His heart with their refusal to hear His teaching. In His youthful humility, Jesus has not yet realised the depth and uniqueness of His understanding of the Father, yet even at twelve, He is consumed by the desire to teach.

Jesus is the supreme Teacher. It was His life's work, to teach us about the Father, to teach us how to love one another, to teach us how to take up our cross and follow Him. Again and again in the Gospels we find His teaching misunderstood even by His own chosen apostles. They at least 'believed', though with varying degrees of confidence, that He "came from God". Others who would hear Him teach, from this youthful period in the Temple right up to this end of His life, would be "filled with amazement". A typical reaction seems to have been: "How did this man get His education when He had no teacher?" Jesus must have been well aware, comparing His own inner certainties with the learned arguments of the scribes and Pharisees, that He did not have what His society considered an 'education'. What He taught came not from books, as we can see even from this icon of His youth, but from Himself. Yet Jesus was emphatic that His teaching did not, in fact, come from Himself in any personal sense: it came from the Father, who communicated it to His Son. "My teaching is not my own; it comes from Him who sent Me". The young Jesus is just starting out on His mission of teaching. We could almost say that the Temple incident is a false start, in that He went back quietly to Nazareth, and waited many years until He felt the time was right for His public mission. During those years, years of learning about the world in which He lived, He must have been drawn more and more deeply into His 'real world, the world of His Father'. Long, silent hours of prayer were the preface to His inspired and impassioned teaching. Jesus looked at His Father, and understood. He came, not only to teach us in words, but to teach us this attitude of prayer. Non-verbally, just by what He is, Jesus urges us to be still and silent and look with Him at the Father.

His years of moving around Galilee, drawing the crowds and teaching them, gathering His apostles and teaching them, would be years of painful effort. Never again, as far as we can judge, would He know the joy that the young Jesus felt in the Temple, when it clearly seemed easy and natural to talk of His Father and to be understood (as expected). He seems not to notice the glowering of the doctors, their obvious hesitation in accepting what He is saying. He is too wrapped, poor lamb, in the wonder of feeling He is among those who 'understand'.

22

4.
The Baptism of Christ

Mid 16th century,
National Art Museum of Ukraine,
Kiev.

4. THE BAPTISM OF CHRIST
Mid 16th century

4. The Baptism of Christ
Mid 16th century

In the Western Church the baptism of Jesus is not considered one of the major feasts. The Eastern Church, however, regards it as a great Epiphany, the first manifestation to the adult Jesus of His Sonship. The first epiphany at His birth, to the Magi, is dim in comparison with the revelation that took place at His baptism. There are countless icons of this numinous event, all honouring the same iconography. Never fully stated, there is a constant reference to His Resurrection descent into the underworld, there to break the powers of Hell and begin His redemptive mission. Here He descends into the waters of the Jordan, which the Eastern theologians called "a liquid sepulchre". Just as He will later rise from the tomb, so He will rise from the waters, radiant with divinity. At the top of the icon we can see the rocks splitting as Jesus descent into the waters. Above Him hovers the dove of the Holy Spirit and the voice of the Father is heard: "You are my beloved Son, in You I am well pleased". This revelation of the Trinity, overwhelming in itself, is perhaps balanced by the human presence of John the Baptist on one side of Jesus, and the angelic presence on the other, suggesting His two natures: God and Man. Apart from a loin cloth that may recall the shroud in which Jesus is buried, He is naked, as befits the new Adam, the one totally free. The angels wait to clothe Him "with the garment of salvation". There are three angels in honour of the Trinity and their hands are veiled.

Covering the hands has always been a mark of reverence for the Eucharist, and this naked Jesus presents Himself to us as Eucharist, He is Thanksgiving incarnate. He is our "Yes" to the Father.

For the world, for us, this is a revelation of the divinity of Jesus. What might it have been for Jesus Himself? We can never enter into the psyche of our Blessed Lord, any more than we can enter into the psyche of our neighbour, however dear to us. We cannot know what He was thinking or what emotions He was experiencing. Yet, it seems to me, this dramatic moment must have come as a supreme confirmation of what He had perhaps only intuited in prayer. It came at a moment of humiliation. Jesus had stripped Himself, joined the throng of sinners waiting to be baptised, and stepped down into the waters without any evidence that this lowly action would provided such an epiphany of God's glory. The icon painter sees the waters as moving of their own accord as they come into contact with the blessed body of Jesus. From now on His blessing will transform water and give it a new significance. That roiling of the waters of itself would have alerted Him to the extraordinary nature of what was to come. Yet, who could have anticipated it: the voice of God Himself acclaiming Jesus, the Holy Spirit hovering over Him in blessing? The Gospel writers differ slightly as to what God actually said. St Matthew has the voice proclaiming to the people, "This is my beloved Son". St Mark and St Luke are more personal. The Divine Voice speaks directly to the Divine Son: "You are my beloved Son. In You I am well pleased". However certain Jesus was of His Sonship, and whatever His confidence that He was doing the will of His Father, ("I do always the things that please Him"), there must still have been an element of ecstatic gratitude in this unmistakable affirmation.

That affirmation was personal to Jesus. As such, we do not share in it, but since He has given Himself to us, we share in that sonship through Him. Because of Jesus, we are certain that God is "Our Father". It cost Him His life to make that certainty our own, and there is deep theological wisdom in showing the baptism as another earlier form of His "descent into hell". He went down into death for us, as He went down into the waters, shattered the rocks and drew us up into the glory of His redemption.

5.
The Miracle of Cana

1315-1321,
Monastery of Chora, Kariyecami,
Istanbul, Turkey.

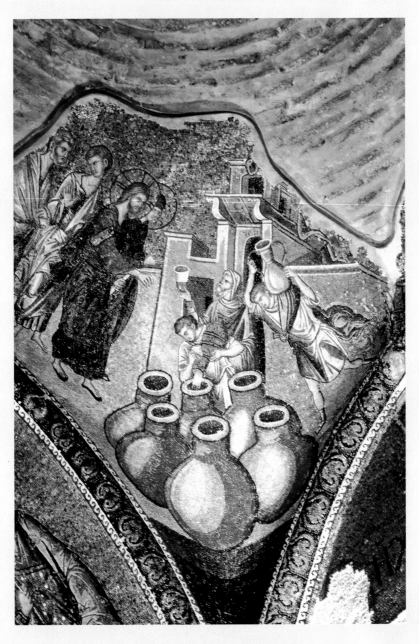

5. THE MIRACLE OF CANA
1315-1321

5. The Miracle of Cana
1315-1321

The first miracle that Jesus worked was unlike any that would follow it. He was prodded into it almost against His will, by His mother's instance, and the occasion seems, to the high minded, relatively insignificant. Jesus, His mother and His disciples had been invited to a wedding. Sometime during the feast, Mary realised that the wine was running out. She turned, as she must so often have done, to her Son "Son, they have no wine". Jesus clearly felt that it was inappropriate to begin His apostolate of the Kingdom by miraculously rescuing a young couple from embarrassment. He tells her, "My time has not yet come". But His mother sees that His time has come, and ignoring His demurrals, calls to the waiters that they should do whatever He tells them. One can imagine Jesus getting up with a sigh, and realising that His Father's will would often be revealed, for Him as for us, in the ordinary circumstances of life. He tells the waiters to fill the great pots with water. These are, in fact, exceedingly great pots, which is all part of the inner significance of this miracle. As we know, the chief steward tastes the water-made-wine and is astonished by its quality. Usually, as he points out, the good wine is served first and the poor stuff is left to the end. This miraculous wine is "the best": one can only imagine what God created at His Son's request! This icon, taken from a mosaic, shows the steward amazed and almost disbelieving, holding up a goblet of this extraordinary wine.

These huge, bulbous water pots loom large in the image: because this miracle has a deeper dimension. Jesus is saving a young couple from the social shame of an inadequate wedding feast. That was local and temporary. What is universal and eternal, is this image of the largess of God's grace. He does not merely provide the few bottles necessary for the feast. He gives lavishly, excessive amounts and all of the most superb quality. We see the waiters hastening with their small, human jugs, to fill up these great, majestic containers in which God will work His miracle.

God is the most abundant and generous of Fathers. However meagre our life experience may be, however diminished by suffering or curtailed by circumstances, the poverty of life is fleeting. We are called to the great banquet of God's fullness in heaven, to the eternal marriage feast, when all is joy and fulfilment. A normal life – since ecstasy is not normal – will never know the overwhelming experience of God's immense and superabundance of goodness. In the icon, Jesus is summoning forth an image of it, a faint metaphor of what it will be like in heaven. The steward and his waiters are engaged in the mechanics of the miracle. Only Jesus and His mother are aware of the sublime significance. But it is not the mechanics that matter, it is the significance, the truth. We may not see, we may be too small to see, "what God has prepared for those who love Him", but we are called to believe in it. We may drink the thin, tepid water of earth, but we believe, because of Jesus, that what awaits us is the rich and glorious wine of heaven.

6.
The Transfiguration

1403, Theophanes the Greek,
Tretyakov Gallery,
Moscow.

6. THE TRANSFIGURATION
Theophanes the Greek

6. The Transfiguration

Theophanes the Greek

The Orthodox Church saw the baptism of Christ as an Epiphany. But the great Epiphany, overshadowing all others, was the Transfiguration. This was not an Epiphany of the Trinity as such, but of the essential divinity of Jesus. For once, He let His glory shine forth, becoming incandescent with a holy light. It is the tradition that an icon painter should always begin his life's work by first painting an icon of the Transfiguration, so that the light of Tabor, that holy blessed light, would illumine everything that the artist would subsequently paint. It was only three apostles who Jesus chose to witness this transcendent experience: Peter, James and John. He took them apart and led them up Mount Tabor, a mountain which has been considered sacred from the earliest times. While the three looked on, wondering, Jesus suddenly blazed forth into a dazzling radiance of light. Illumined by this light, on either side of Him, appeared the forms of Moses and Elijah; Moses the great law giver, Elijah the great prophet. In this extraordinary icon we can see at the top corners the angels who have brought the prophets from heaven to converse with Jesus. Not only is it a vision of the glory that is of the essence of the Saviour, but this icon also sets this glory firmly in a Trinitarian context. Three great rays of bluish light fall on the apostles from the white blue aureole that encircles Jesus. Such glory, such theological significance, completely overwhelms the three humble men who have ascended the mountain quite unsuspectingly. Peter on the left falls back, overcome, yet he is the only one who is still able to look up at Jesus, however dazed and uncomprehending. John in the middle has collapsed, seemingly breathless, while James, equally overcome, closes his eyes, unable to bear the intensity of the light. The icon painter sets in two small scenes at centre left and right, one showing Jesus leading the apostles up the mountain, and the other showing him leading them down. They were told not to speak of what they had seen, but it is clear why they had been privileged with such an extraordinary vision. These are the three who Jesus would choose to keep Him company in the Garden of Olives, where He was to agonise over His coming death. This piercing glimpse of who Jesus really is, the Son of God, should strengthen them against the distress of seeing His human weakness. There is another link to the Passion: the Gospels tell us that Jesus spoke to Moses and Elijah about His coming Passion.

Announcements of the Passion were precisely what the Apostles did not want to hear. Peter speaks for all of them when he begs that they may be allowed to stay on Mount Tabor. The gospel adds kindly "he did not know what he was saying". He knew what he wanted, which is what we all want, to live in the glory and the bliss, to have faith made easy because we can see the divinity of Jesus. But Tabor is short lived. Jesus will lead the apostles down, back into the troubles and difficulties of their real world, a world in which the Son of God will be crucified. One of the most moving lines in scripture is the description of what the apostles see when Jesus dims His radiance and Moses and Elijah return to heaven. We are told that looking up "they saw no one, only Jesus". This could be taken as the perfect description of the dedicated Christian.

7.
Prayer of Petition

17th century, Greek or Cretan,
Temple Gallery,
London.

7. PRAYER OF PETITION
17th century Greek or Cretan

7. Prayer of Petition
17th century Greek or Cretan

This icon seems to me to spell out the function of prayer of petition. It is an unusual subject, and we do not know the names of the man who prays or of the Saint to whom his prayer is addressed. What we can see however, very clearly, is how prayer 'works'. The man in black prays passionately for a miracle. We can see what is causing him such anguish: three people, obviously dear to him, are in danger of drowning. Opposed to the pleading sinner on his knees, in penitential black, stands the radiant figure of a saint, hardly here on earth at all, one foot raised as if to ascend back to heaven. But the saint is in touch with heaven, communicates with heaven (this is what it means to be a saint) and he directs the prayer to the only one who can answer it, Jesus Himself. No saint can work a miracle: it is Jesus who works the miracle. The kneeling man has done all he can to make his prayer acceptable. He has withdrawn from the city, which we can see in the far distance, and has disciplined his will, as evidenced by his dark clothing. He has enlisted the help of a saint in whom he trusts. Both saint and sinner lift pleading hands, Jesus stretches out blessing and welcoming hands, and down below the three, who have almost drowned, lift up their hands in gratitude.

The whole cycle is here. We do what we can to pray, as Jesus would want us to pray. He hears our prayer. He answers it.

During His life on earth, we see again and again how the compassion of Jesus urged Him to perform miracles. He often asked that the miracle could be a secret, as if well aware of the expectations it might arouse. Miracles, events inexplicable by normal standards, are not the norm. When we pray, even if it is for a miracle, we are wise not to expect a literal response. There will always be a response, even if we do not get our petition granted. One cry from the heart, and Jesus comes down to us, to stand with us, to make the unbearable possible. We can see in the icon how close the Lord is to His unhappy supplicant. In the icon, a miracle has been granted, but even had it not been, there still would have been succour and support for the unhappy man who so longs to be heard.

8.
The Parable
of the Widow's Mite

1500-1502, Dionysius and his sons,
The Church of the Nativity of the Virgin,
Ferapontov Monastery, Russia.

8. THE PARABLE OF THE WIDOW'S MITE
Dionysius and his sons

8. The Parable of the Widow's Mite
Dionysius and his sons

This is a very rare icon, and the fresco in the Ferapantov Monastery, by the great Dionysius, is sadly faded. Yet, it still retains its interior power. Jesus and His Apostles – we can see them in the icon clustered behind Him – have been in the Temple in Jerusalem, watching the great and lordly put generous sums into the offertory bowl. The iconographer suggests that these rich men are well aware of the amount of their donations, and are well satisfied to be seen as devout. But what strikes the attention of Jesus is the offering made by a poor widow. She shyly places in the bowl the tiniest of coins: a mite. By worldly standards this is a donation hardly to be noticed. In our relatively wealthy society, there is no coin as small as a 'mite'. We can imagine the contempt with which those who see her action regard such a meagre sacrifice. Perhaps the Apostles too are raising cynical eyebrows at such apparent lack of generosity. But Jesus turns to them. He tells them that the rich have given out of their abundance: they will hardly notice their donation. But this poor widow has given "all that she had, her livelihood". Dionysius or perhaps his sons, picture her as very slender. The intention was almost certainly to show her as thin and hungry as opposed to the well-fed gentlemen who are behind her in the queue. It is an amazing revelation of the ardour of first century Jewish faith. This solitary woman was prepared to deprive herself so that she could honour God's Temple.

Jesus is making two points to His disciples. The first is that we cannot judge by what we see. She seems to others to be giving almost nothing. In reality she was giving more than anybody else. Not judging is a fundamental of Jesus' teaching. He stresses, again and again, that, in fact, we cannot judge: we do not know the heart. Only God can judge, and this may be for the better or for the worse. What looks impressive may be simply conceit. We are showing off. In God's eyes, this is not generosity but self-seeking. Equally, what we might sneer at, God sees as a great act of loving self-denial. That may well have been the major lesson Jesus wanted to teach. But secondly, He is also teaching the beauty of self sacrifice, seen by none, visible and loved by God alone. This acting in solitude, indifferent to opinions of our neighbours, is again a fundamental of Jesus' teaching. We must look to the Father, only to the Father, and do what is right.

What I find especially touching in this little story, is that Jesus did not speak to the widow. We can see in the icon, how his head is turned back, away from her, speaking to His disciples. She never knew that on the day she humbly placed in the bowl 'her livelihood', that the Son of God had seen her and loved her and used her self sacrifice as an example to His followers.

9.
Christ at the Well

20th century,
Aidan Hart.

CHRIST AT THE WELL

9. CHRIST AT THE WELL
Aidan Hart

9. Christ at the Well

Aidan Hart

The gospels are so intent upon the meaning of Jesus, and the transforming significance of His teaching, that they give us very few personal details. We know that Jesus was fully human, with a history and a body and a personality, but it is not often that we are shown this in practice. That is one of the special qualities that make the incident of Jesus at the well memorable.

Jesus and the Apostles were travelling through Samaria and before they reached the little town of Sychar, Jesus was so exhausted that He could go no further. He sent the Apostles into the city to forage for bread: Aidan Hart shows the small rounded enclosure of Sychar behind the mountains that bar easy access to it. This human Jesus, not only exhausted and hungry, but thirsty too, sits down on the well outside the gates. Probably, in a dry land like Samaria, all wells were sacred, but this was a special well, this was Jacob's well. The story tells how a Samaritan woman comes to draw water. Normally, a decent man and decent woman found alone would not converse together. Still more a devout Jew would not speak to a heretical Samaritan, but Jesus takes no notice of cultural conditioning. With divine simplicity, He asks this foreign woman for a drink. The icon shows her astonishment, accosted by a man, and even more, accosted by a Jew, those despisers of Samaritans. She is not even in reality a 'decent woman'. As Jesus knows with His divine insight, she is a very much-married lady, and her present 'husband' is not married to her at all. This is precisely the kind of person a good Jew would avoid at all costs. But Jesus sees to the heart, that heart which like all human hearts, longs for God, despite the foolishness and muddle of their actual lives. He asks her for water, courteously giving her the chance to be the giver. Then He tells her that He too has a gift, that of "living water". "Whoever drinks of this water will never thirst".

Aiden Hart shows how the presence of Jesus stirs the natural waters of the well: they move in response to the electricity of the Divine Presence. The woman, whose name is never given, does not understand, but she knows she is in the presence of the Holy, and she is filled with desire for this mysterious 'living water'. When she leaves Jesus, and hurries back to the city with her tidings, the Samaritan authorities disregard her. A woman of such loose morals is not to be accepted as a true witness: they will believe only if they themselves meet Jesus.

This is typical of Jesus, to see beneath the surface, to choose as His messenger a woman that others so readily can despise. He has a longer conversation with her than with almost anyone else in the scriptures, and His words about the living water still resound throughout the centuries. It was St Teresa of Avila, that great Carmelite mystic and now a Doctor of the Church, who came closest to understanding what Jesus meant. She saw how water came to us in so many ways, river water, well water, artesian water, rain water... all were symbols of prayer. It is when we drink the living water that we are taken into Jesus, and that water is always there for us: it is a symbol of His presence. However small our human jug, (look at the little vessel which the woman has brought to the well), the well of the living water is infinite, alive with the Lord.

What I always love about this icon is that the woman too is given a halo. She might have been a most disreputable character, but she came close to Jesus. She listened to Him. In that very contact, she was being changed into a different woman, a holy woman, anonymous but never to be forgotten, (the Orthodox Church calls her St Protini). This is what prayer will always do, it will change us.

10.
The Raising of Lazarus

Byzantine,
Benaki Museum,
Athens.

10. THE RAISING OF LAZARUS
Byzantine

10. The Raising of Lazarus
Byzantine

The raising of Lazarus was Jesus' last and greatest miracle. It was the only one done for a friend, because we are told Jesus 'loved Lazarus', and He was certainly fond of his two sisters Martha and Mary. When He knew that Lazarus was dying, Jesus steeled Himself to ignore the tearful pleas of his sisters, but we are told that He Himself was greatly distressed. Lazarus is dead: he has been three days shrouded in the tomb. It is only now that Jesus comes to Bethany, all hope gone, as Martha reproachfully reminds him, "if you had been here our brother would not have died". This is great faith. Yet she is speaking to one who can say of Himself, "I am the resurrection and the life, whoever believes in me will never die". In this extraordinary miracle, Jesus proves His words. The raising of Lazarus is like a parable, spelling out, in physical form, the spiritual significance of faith.

As told in the Gospel, this is a crowded scene. The apostles are there, pressing around Jesus, half believing, half fearing. Mary and Martha are there, on their knees. The Pharisees and scribes, the enemies of Jesus, have come out from the city, to witness the failure of His extravagant boast. The gravediggers are there, very unwilling to open the tomb. As is bluntly pointed out, after three days, in the Palestinian heat, a corpse will have putrefied, and the odour would be horrific.

All the drama is concentrated on the two figures, Jesus making the lordly gesture as He recalls His dead friend to life, and a friend still enshrouded in his burial garment, rising to his feet, white amidst the darkness of death.

This is not really a story about recalling Lazarus to life. It is a story about recalling the dead soul to the life of God, through faith. Even the hostile Pharisees are astonished. One raises his hand in amazement, but the other stretches out to Jesus the open hand of belief. Has he come to believe? In a very short time, Jesus Himself will descend into the darkness of death (and the excitement caused by this miracle will be used by His enemies against Him). When He descends Himself into the pit, Jesus will split the rocks asunder, and bring about the salvation of all humankind. The strangely contoured rocks in the background are surely meant to remind us of that coming death and that glorious resurrection. Lazarus, despite his splendid halo, (and we notice that he is the only one except Jesus to be so privileged), has not been resurrected. He is as he was before he died. In the course of time he will die again. But because he has been touched by the grace of faith, it will be only his body that will die and rest in the ground until the final universal resurrection.

The icon wants to stress above all the power of Jesus, that His presence transforms even the dead. The resolute sinner, the evil man, if such exists, is totally dead: him too, the grace of Jesus can bring back to life, spiritual life. But everybody in this picture, including ourselves, and excluding Jesus, is partly dead, in that we are not like Him, totally given to the Father. The icon strives to awaken our longing for that total surrender that is eternal life.

11.
Entrance into Jerusalem

18th century Romanian,
Temple Gallery,
London.

11. ENTRANCE INTO JERUSALEM
18th century Romanian

11. Entrance into Jerusalem

18th century Romanian

The entry of Jesus into Jerusalem, commonly known as Palm Sunday, is one of the great feasts of the Church. This Sunday is the beginning of Holy Week, a week that will end on Good Friday with the death of Jesus and be climaxed by Easter Sunday a week later. On this Sunday, Jesus, for the first time, made a solemn entrance into Jerusalem. He had come up for the Passover, as He had done many times before, but this was to be the culmination of His life's work, and He approached the city, not humbly on foot as usual but riding on a donkey.

Official visits to a city, by an emperor or some high dignitary, were occasions for a civic procession. The emperor would ride in, the officials would greet him, the people would applaud. When Jesus enters Jerusalem, it is almost in parody of such imperial pomp. He wears simple clothes, He carries no sceptre but holds the book of the Bible, His steed is a rather insignificant donkey. Above all he is seated side-saddle, as if resting on the donkey rather than controlling him. His retinue is only His faithful apostles. They do not quite know what to make of this gesture. Jesus has enemies in the city: is it wise for Him, even in this lowly fashion, to draw attention to Himself? Peter leans towards Jesus dangling an anachronistic key, hands held wide in expostulation. Other apostles behind him echo this gesture of entreaty.

The icon painter, who is not of the most sophisticated, carefully labels every halo which has managed to wedge itself into the picture. At the entrance to the city, elderly Jews wave branches, with rather unambiguous lack of enthusiasm. The gospel story is actually more exuberant than the icon reveals, with shouts of Hosanna and garments thrown beneath Jesus' feet. It is possible that the brown smudges at the bottom of the icon are intended to represent these marks of tribute. What makes this icon so appealing is the look on the Lord's face. He is half-smiling, wholly benign, His long and beautiful countenance gleaming with the light of His divinity. This day of seeming triumph must have been a bittersweet experience for Him. Within a few days the crowds that acclaim Him would be urging Pilate to crucify Him. Jesus looks neither to the apostles nor to the city officials, although He lifts His hand in blessing. He seems to be looking within, aware only of the Father, and wryly cognisant of the ephemeral nature of popularity. He does not wish men and women to accept Him on a great surge of emotion. That will not last. The true 'Hosanna' can spring only from a heart that chooses, whatever the emotions, to believe and to trust. Jesus is riding, or rather being carried, to what He knows is His death. He accepts what is to come as the inevitable result of who He is. There is grace in abundance for all who will accept it, but He is sadly aware that there will be few. Even the donkey droops his head compassionately.

12.
Jesus Washes the Feet
of the Disciples

13th century,
St Catherine's Monastery,
Mount Sinai, Egypt.

12. JESUS WASHES THE FEET OF THE DISCIPLES
13th century

12. Jesus Washes the Feet of the Disciples
13th century

At the Last Supper, before they sat down together, Jesus washed the disciples' feet. They were astonished, altogether taken aback. Peter, as usual, voiced the general dismay "Lord, You will never wash my feet!" In dusty Palestine it was customary to have one's dirty feet washed before a meal, but it was the job of a servant, or in Roman households, a slave. It was inconceivable to the Apostles that Jesus Himself, their "Lord and Master", should do something so menial. They are almost angry and Jesus wants to show them that this violent reaction comes from a misunderstanding of what it is to be 'servant'. Everyone is called upon to be a servant, metaphorically to wash the feet of others. There is no indignity in it. In fact, it is part of the dignity of being a Christian, that we serve our neighbour in whatever way is needed, and that our own 'importance' counts for nothing. Unless we are self-forgetful, unless we think of others' needs, we are not followers of Jesus. This scene, the washing of the feet, has been depicted on stone tombs and in manuscripts from the 6th century on. It was clearly seen that humility was essential to what Jesus was and what He taught.

Here, there is even more to it. The Apostles are being washed in preparation for their receiving of the body and blood of the Lord. When Peter objects to having his feet washed, Jesus tells him that no one can have "part of Him", unless they are "clean". The icon shows Peter distressed by this gentle rebuke, offering to be washed from head down, while Jesus explains that the feet are enough. Washing of our busy feet, so active and so necessary to all we do, is a symbol of the desire to be pure. This 'washing' is an acted parable, illuminating the meaning of the Sacrament of Reconciliation, where we let Jesus wash us, take us into His own holiness, and so make us ready to receive the gifts that His Father longs to give. Notice how the other Apostles are fully clad and upright, as opposed to Peter, seated on the stool of penitence, vulnerable and exposed. Jesus trains the whole force of His loving compassion on His humbled, abashed Peter. He can wash Peter, He can purify him to the depth of his heart, because Peter is willing, however reluctantly, to accept that he is dirty and that God's grace must cleanse him.

There are two lessons in humility here. The first is that we must subordinate ourselves to the needs of others. The second, which maybe harder, is to accept that we need cleansing. People can beat their breast about their sinfulness and feel that they are very aware of their need for grace. Emotional contrition, however, is merely the first step toward actually doing something about it. The act of washing, or rather of being washed, is a very simple one: it is also, for most people, difficult. In practical terms, it is the Sacrament of Reconciliation that does for the repentant Christian what Jesus is here doing for the Apostles. It is Jesus who brings forward the bowl of water. It is Jesus who urges us to sit on the stool of penitence. It is Jesus who, with infinite love, listens to our faltering confession on how we have failed Him. There is only joy and gratitude in this Sacrament, and here we see Peter entering into the mystery of the love of God, fresh, clean, made ready.

13.
Communion of the Apostles

Early 17th century,
Temple Gallery,
London.

13. COMMUNION OF THE APOSTLES
Early 17th century

13. Communion of the Apostles
Early 17th century

This icon is also called the "Liturgical Eucharist", and it is not set in the realistic context of the Last Supper meal. Every Mass commemorates the Last Supper, in a sense is the Last Supper, and the icon is showing not so much what happened in history, but what happens in eternity. Jesus is standing within an early Christian church. The altar is covered with a red cloth, as was often customary, and over the altar is a sheltering architectural canopy known as a ciborium. Today a ciborium refers to the holy container that protects the consecrated hosts, and this protecting canopy has the same function of reverence. Often there were two icons of The Communion, with six Apostles on either side, so this icon probably had a companion. Jesus has said the words of consecration and the large bowl He holds out no longer contains wine but, mystically, is His Body and His Blood. This is, of course, a mystery that no human mind can fathom. What it means to "take and eat", "take and drink", is a truth that we will only begin to comprehend when the limitations of this life are over. We live by the Eucharist, but we live in an absolute of faith. We see nothing, we taste nothing, but we know with complete certainty that we are being given the total Jesus who gave Himself at the Last Supper. The Apostles' faith must have been great indeed, because it was Jesus Himself, so alive and present before them, who said those bewildering words and offered that astonishing invitation. Here, standing behind the little altar with its significant cross, Jesus lovingly welcomes these first believers. Peter bends low, to sip from the chalice. John is behind him and we can see from the swirl of his robes, that he has been running, eager and longing to come close to his Lord. The others crane forward, wondering and reverent. How could they understand? Jesus did not ask them to understand, only to receive. In the long, lonely years ahead, this little group of followers will learn the effect of the Eucharist.

Without the Mass there is no Church. It is receiving the true Jesus, surrendered to His Father in the Eucharist, that makes it possible for us to be surrendered. On our own, what power would we have, weak and tempted as we are? The Church has made Sunday Mass obligatory, simply because this is something we desperately need. Receiving Holy Communion, (which, of course, we can do every day and not only on a Sunday), is our purest act of faith. Going up to the altar and receiving the small host is a lived expression of our trust in the Father. Our part is to come to that Eucharist with desire, not necessarily a felt desire or an experience of longing, but a rational desire. We accept that the Eucharist is Jesus Himself, and that the bodily reception of this Sacrament draws us out of our helplessness and smallness into the pure goodness of God. Jesus is that goodness made visible. It was made visible, in the body, to the Apostles: it is made visible to us in faith. When we cannot receive Holy Communion, we should live in desire for it, believing that this is our great chance to be taken into Jesus.

14.
The Agony in the Garden

Contemporary

14. THE AGONY IN THE GARDEN
Contemporary

14. The Agony in the Garden
Contemporary

T his is a detail from a contemporary icon of the Agony in the Garden. But there is no garden here. Jesus is cramped into a small and rocky space: this is an instance where the constriction incidental to a detail has a symbolic function. In the story, as we know from the Gospels, Jesus withdrew into the Garden of Gethsemani after the Last Supper. He had often spent the night in prayer, alone, but this was the night before His passion, and He felt the need for human support. He brought with Him His three closest friends, Peter, James and John, and asked them "to watch with Him". They did not watch, they fell asleep. Obviously, these men loved Jesus but equally so, they could not imagine that He would have a real emotional need of them. Surely Jesus only needed His Father? But Jesus was fully human, and this was the night in which His human vulnerability was fully displayed. The Apostles saw only His courage and His Faith: they left their Master alone. This icon shows Jesus in His loneliness. No iconographer could ever bring himself to depict, as western artists can, the utter physical desolation of Jesus on this night. With every fibre of His holy being, He shrank from death, not only the pain of it, but for all it meant of failure in His mission to reveal the Father. This wonderful image, Jesus clothed in a blood red garment, shows Him stretching forth His hands to that invisible Father. He is both pleading for rescue ("take this cup away from Me") and offering His total submission, ("but if I must drink it your will be done").

So often those who write about the saints stress their indifference to suffering. Sometimes, we are even told of their joy in suffering. They seem never to know fear or even anxiety: they glory in the cross. This can be deeply discouraging for those of us who are well acquainted with fear and anxiety, who shrink from pain and have to steel themselves to accept with love even the lightest of crosses. It may well be true that holy men and women have desired to suffer, but it is not a natural desire, nor one Jesus Himself experienced. All His teaching made it clear that the Father wants us to relish life: "I have come that they have life, life to the full". Jesus used His life, in all the ways that His vocation made possible, He delighted in the flowers, He noticed the birds, He enjoyed parties, or so we may deduce from the criticism of the Pharisees. When he saw people suffering, His heart was moved with compassion. His was a life of frequent sorrows, longing as He did for His beloved people to understand the Fatherhood of God, and live in freedom. He met rejection, even, at the end, a semi-rejection from His chosen Apostles. Part of this agony in Gethsemani must have been His knowledge that they did not understand, that they were leaving Him alone in His anguish, and that they would all run away when He was arrested. The iconographer shows us the dignity of Jesus in His grief. He is shut in by the hard, jagged reality of His future, He longs with all His heart for it to be different, but He stretches out in loving acceptance to the Father in whom He trusts.

There is no joy here, but infinite grace for all of us who want to be like Him.

15.
Christ Before Pilate

Early 16th century,
Temple Gallery,
London.

15. CHRIST BEFORE PILATE
Early 16th century

15. Christ Before Pilate

Early 16th century

C hrist before Pilate is one of great confrontations of history. In fact, it is 'the confrontation', the only time when the pure power of the Spirit, incarnate, faced the pure power of the world. Pilate represented the greatest secular power that humanity was to know for many centuries. He represents Rome, but equally he represents Hitler and Fascism, Stalin and Mao and Communism. He represents Imperial America and will one day be a representative of Imperial India or South America or wherever the centre of the world's authority exists. He is Authority, and he is well aware of it. Over his head is the scarlet canopy of Imperial might and he is dressed appropriately for his rank. The solidity of the architectural background is symbolic of all the armies and treasuries and judicial courts that back up his position.

In this sense Jesus has no power: He has nothing material behind Him. As He tells Pilate, "My kingdom is not of this world". In becoming human, the Son of God has chosen to become 'a common man'. He is poor, living His life in a small, unimportant country, unable to impose His Will. Power is all about imposing one's will: Jesus forgoes this. He will never force. He wants followers who will choose to obey, who will use their freewill to reach out of their creaturely inadequacies to the transforming love of God. Here He has been brought before Pilate, as a condemned criminal: lowest of the low. Jesus will not accept the untruth of this. He is no criminal, and He defies Pilate to find a moral justification for his condemnation. On the other hand, Jesus is fully aware that 'authority' has been given to Pilate, in a worldly sense, and He is gently challenging this Roman governor to think for himself and make decisions according to his own conscience. To follow Jesus is to live in freedom. All that we do we choose to do: all that we believe, we accept and ratify. There is a terrible irony in seeing the barefoot Son of God bowing respectfully before a worldly authority, one that He is quite ready to accept as long as it is exercised within its moral bounds. Earlier on in His life, He had said that, "we must render to Caesar the things that are Caesar's and to God, the things that are God's".

Because Jesus is quite unconcerned with how He seems and of His own 'status' (what does it matter?), He sees no indignity in showing respect for Pilate. The more we share in the humility of Jesus, the more free we are to allow others their own importance. But He cannot allow external authority to regulate His choices, choices made in the light of conscience (He knows what His Father asks of Him).

We grieve to see Our Lord sent to His death by a weak and venal authority. All the countless multitudes who have been persecuted and misjudged throughout history find Jesus standing beside them.

16.
The Holy Face

20th century, Monk Gregory Kroug,
Three Saints Church,
Paris.

16. THE HOLY FACE
Monk Gregory Kroug

16. The Holy Face

Monk Gregory Kroug

Sometimes the expression: 'not made with hands' is used for icons of Our Lady thought to be painted by St Luke, (who certainly had hands). Its true designation, however, is the mysterious image of Jesus that was said to be miraculously imprinted on a cloth that touched His face. It was the most sacred icon of Byzantium, it was called the mandylion, and it vanished in the destruction of Constantinople in the Middle Ages. There is a copy in the Vatican, and it has been faithfully reproduced over the centuries. The western legend speaks of an image imprinted on the towel that St Veronica (*vera icon*, the true icon) offered Jesus on His way to the cross. He wiped His face and handed her the cloth now showing this icon. The eastern legend has the King of Edessa, Abgar, sending a messenger to Jesus to bring Him to Syria to heal the King. Jesus did not come but pressed a cloth to His face and gave the miraculous image to take back. There are many icons depicting that same holy face; this is one by a contemporary Russian artist, a priest, highly influential in reviving the true tradition of the icon. The monk Gregory escaped from Russia and served His Lord in France. Here is a grave-eyed Jesus, His face marked by suffering. This Jesus is aware only of the Father. Monk Gregory shows Him pallid, exhausted on his way to the cross, his gaze fixed within. He delicately outlines a simple cloth or towel on which that holy face was imprinted. All that matters is that the artist and we who look upon the image, are in the presence of Jesus.

It must have been overwhelming in those early centuries of the Faith, to feel that this was truly the face of the Saviour, a face not painted but expressed in material form by the power of God Himself. It was "not made with human hands". That early, original icon may be lost, but the face of Jesus can never be one "made with hands". His face is imprinted in our hearts. It is loving Him that draws us into an awareness of His holy Face. This most beautiful icon is a reminder to us of that inward image that we cannot see and yet will impress itself, if we allow it, on every aspect of our life. The true icon is created from the prayer and love of the iconographer. But it cannot stop there. It draws those who contemplate it into that same love, that same desire to have what St Paul called "the mind of Christ". As Christians, we have been imprinted with His image. It is the great sorrow of God that the sacred icon within us is so often left inert. There is nothing superficial about the reality of the Holy Face of our Saviour and the more we pray before it, the more we are drawn into its truth.

17.
The Crucifixion

8th century,
St Catherine's Monastery,
Mount Sinai, Egypt.

17. THE CRUCIFIXION
8th century

17. The Crucifixion

8th century

I t took the Church a long time to accept the physical reality of the crucifixion. Not only was it a painful death, and those who loved Jesus shrank from its full brutality, but it was also a degrading death. No Roman citizen could be crucified (that is why when St Paul and St Peter were martyred in Rome, only St Peter was crucified; St Paul as a Roman citizen had the privilege of decapitation). At first, and reluctantly, only the bare cross was shown, without any figure. But, by the 5th and 6th centuries, the memory of what crucifixion really meant faded, and the Church acknowledged the truth. But these early icons of the crucifixion shows Jesus in His majesty. He triumphs over the cross, seemingly invulnerable, despite the nails and the blood. In this powerful, damaged and very early image, the Church has advanced, at least, to an image of Jesus dead. His arms may still be stretched out, straight and powerful. His feet may still seem to rest solidly on the cross bar. His body does not slump. But His eyes are closed. That strong and beautiful face is at rest in death.

Around the dead but triumphant Jesus is the full assembly of those who were witnesses of this, the greatest event of human history. Above His head angels grieve. They not only grieve, they lift their hands in astonishment and awe. The mystery of the human rejection of their Saviour leaves them breathless. On either side of the angels would have been sun and moon: the icon is not complete it has been injured by time. Below that, equally fragmented, would have been the two thieves, one of whom accepted Jesus, one of whom died blaspheming. The look of patient love on Jesus' face leads one to hope that both these sinners came to salvation, one while he was dying and the other in death when he saw the truth of God. Then we come to those who stood faithfully by Him, His mother Mary and the disciple whom He loved, John. Both stand grieving and dignified, entering into His pain but also into its meaning. Finally, minuscule at the foot of the cross, are the Roman soldiers dicing for His garments. The indifference to the realities of proportion is typical of the 8th century and for centuries to come. Holy people were always shown as very large. As we can see here, Jesus dominates the picture, Mary and John are smaller but still significant, the thief, representing ordinary sinful humanity, is smaller still, while the soldiers are dwarfed. This expresses a spiritual truth, the importance in God's sight of those in the icon. Although the soldiers, in worldly terms were all powerful, driving in the nails and raising the cross, in the light of eternity they were mere instruments. It is the other three humans who matter, in that they share in the passion and so have their part in the great Redemption.

The iconographer cannot bear to depict Jesus stripped. He is modestly clothed in a long tunic, and yet it is blood stained, and blood pours from His upper side and His pierced feet. Is it significant that the blood and water, which St John describes, seem mostly to be falling onto rock? This noble Jesus has given all. He still holds His hands outstretched, (and blood from the right hand is not wasted, it baptises the repentant thief). Yet those outstretched arms, it seems to us, long to embrace in love the indifferent soldiers who take no notice of the crucifixion. We could feel, even in this unemotional icon, that Jesus dies essentially of a broken heart.

18.
The Descent into Hell

1502-3, Workshop of Dionysius,
Russian Museum,
St Petersburg, Russia.

18. THE DESCENT INTO HELL
Workshop of Dionysius

18. The Descent into Hell
Workshop of Dionysius

For the Orthodox Church, the classic image of the Resurrection is not so much Jesus rising from the tomb, (which is completely unimaginable anyway), but of Jesus descending into hell. Hell here means the 'underworld', where all the dead are waiting for His salvation. At the very top of the icon is the cross worshipped by angels, and making it radiantly clear that it is by His death, by His sacrifice of Himself, that Jesus has broken open the gates of the underworld, of hell. In the centre, translucent and beautiful, stands the resurrected Jesus. He is tugging out from hell His human forebears Adam and Eve. She is in full radiant scarlet because it is woman who gives birth to life, Adam is more subdued, as befits a labourer. Behind Adam stand David and Solomon wearing their crowns, waiting their turn for deliverance. Behind Eve is John the Baptist and, among others, Noah holding a small model of the ark. The gates of hell have been shattered, rising like a drawbridge. Beneath Jesus are the angels imprisoning the Devil who will never again have the power to roam unfettered on the earth. Jesus has conquered him. Behind the glowing angels in the centre, dimly glimpsed in the darkness of the underworld are the vices, each personified by a devil, and each pierced through by a beam of light that comes from the angels who surround Jesus in the blue globe of the world. Each angel and each devil is named: the angel of obedience spears the devil of pride, and the angel of humility spears to death the devil of conceit. Above, where Jesus reigns, all is light; below in the underworld, all is darkness. These supporting details are hard to read with clarity, but what is very clear are the masses of the forgotten dead to right and to left clothed in white and stretching out their hands in love and hope and desire. Them too, all of them, the countless millions, Jesus will rescue from the darkness and lead them into the light of His Father.

The icon is not so much concerned with what happened, that Jesus rose from the dead, but what this meant. It meant that the power of hell had been broken and that heaven was wide open to all who were willing to receive God's love. In one sense, of course, it is all the work of Jesus. He died for us, He saved us, He leads us into happiness. But we must do our small part as well. Adam and Eve, and all the dead lift up their hands so that Jesus may seize them and by His grace transform their state. These dead are blessed in that, in all their lives, they sought the Will of God, and so when Jesus comes to them they want only to receive Him. We are blessed, perhaps even more blessed, in that the work of salvation has been done, and we can lift up our hands while we are still alive. The angels of grace can pierce within us the devils of our sinfulness, not after death but during life. Jesus asks us only to let Him pull us, wrench us if need be, out of the tomb of our selfishness.

Two things are striking in this icon. One is the vigour of Jesus, grace made visible, infinite love and power. The other is the eagerness with which our first parents receive Him. They are saved, drawn into heaven, because they want to be. It is the choice of the will, to obey, to accept the Lord, or to turn selfishly away from Him, that determines our future.

88

19.
Noli Me Tangere

1603, Emmanuel Lambardos,
Museum of Icons,
Dubrovnik, Croatia.

19. NOLI ME TANGERE
Emmanuel Lambardos

19. Noli Me Tangere

Emmanuel Lambardos

The first person to see the risen Jesus was a woman, Mary Magdalene. She had come to the tomb, bearing spices to anoint His body. Here, in the icon, we see the tomb behind her with the grave cloth lying still folded. Mary was distraught to find the empty tomb. She did not notice how the chill of spring had been miraculously vanquished by the olive tree springing into bloom amidst the rocks, and the meadow before it blossoming with unseasonal flowers. She is aware of nothing but of the absence of the One she loves. She thinks she sees the gardener: obviously, her eyes are blinded with tears, because the gardener is Jesus Himself. He speaks to her, Mary. At once she understands what has happened, that Jesus has risen. Death cannot hold Him and in His freedom all humanity has been set free. The icon shows Jesus translucent with the light of His rising, His very garments transfigured. He holds in His hand a roll of parchment (this is not a biblical detail) which legend says contains the full role of human sinfulness, all redeemed by His sacrifice. It is the short and poignant conversation between Mary Magdalene and the risen Jesus that gives this incident its title. She reaches out to Him, longing only to hold Him fast. Jesus has escaped her wants in death. She will not let Him go again. Jesus, gently and lovingly, tells her that she has misunderstood. Union with Him, the risen Jesus, will not be physical. *"Noli me tangere"*. "Do not hold Me". The risen Jesus transcends the material dimension in which we live. We become close to Him, not by holding His outward form, but by loving His inward truth. He goes on to explain: "I have not yet ascended to the Father". This visible Jesus is only temporary. After forty days He will 'ascend' and earth will see Him no more until the Day of Judgement. Mary and the disciples would be wasting their energies if they were to cling to Him as He is now. No, there is an infinitely closer embrace awaiting all who love Him. It will not be in a flower strewn meadow. These paradisal circumstances are only for the great resurrection Sunday. What He is offering is something far deeper and more intimate. He will ascend and send His Holy Spirit, and the Holy Spirit of Jesus will take up His residence within us. We will never need to 'hold Him': it will be He who will always hold us.

This gleaming Jesus, His wounds beautiful with light, all sorrow behind Him, wholly present in the garden: this Jesus we will not see. Unlike Mary Magdalene, our vocation is to live by faith, and to believe in the beauty of God in its holy invisibility.

20.
The Doubting of Thomas

Early 16th century, Novgorod,
The Menil Collection,
Houston.

20. THE DOUBTING OF THOMAS
Novgorod

20. The Doubting of Thomas
Novgorod

Mary Magdalene was the first to see Jesus, in the most ideal of circumstances, (there, alone, in the garden), but she was by no means the last. Although Jesus sent her and the other women to tell the Apostles, so that they would not be unprepared, it was to them above all that He wanted to show Himself. The gospels reveal their amazement and initial incredulity. "They thought they were seeing a ghost". Their fear was enhanced by His miraculous appearance. After the disaster of Calvary, they had hidden themselves away in an Upper Room, a secluded place where they could hide from their enemies and get over the traumatic shock of Jesus' death. They were very careful to shut all the doors. The icon shows us that solid metallic door, through which Jesus passed. His was a Resurrection body. No doors could hinder His freedom. It took the Lord some time and some persuasion before the bewildered Apostles realised that there was no call for mourning but rather for an astonished joy. However, when Jesus appeared to them, one Apostle was missing, Thomas. Thomas regarded their ecstatic description of their experience as a pathetic example of wishful thinking. He knew that Jesus was dead, although it broke the heart to accept it. However earnestly the others assured him that Jesus was not dead, that they had actually seen Him, Thomas was adamant he would not believe. Rather, mockingly, he told them he would believe only if he could see this 'Jesus', and verify the presence of His wounds. He needed to touch them, put his fingers into the hole that the spear had made in His side, before he could accept this seemingly incredible story. A week to the day, "the doors being shut", Jesus materialised again. This time, Thomas was present. One can only imagine the wonder with which he looked upon Jesus come back from the dead. The icon shows Jesus standing on a small rostrum, as if the Apostles had prepared a sacred space in the hope that He would visit them once again. On either side, awed and reverent, stand the Apostles, still overcome by the mystery. Jesus singles out Thomas, who must have been standing speechless in their midst. To all appearances, the Lord had not been present when Thomas made his foolish challenge, yet He had heard it. He tells His doubting follower to come close and to put his finger into the wounds. It must have been a shaming and overwhelming experience for this man whose faith had not been strong enough. Jesus tells him gently, "you believe because you have seen Me Thomas", and then gives us, who have never had this experience, our glorious tribute, "blessed are those who have not seen Me and yet believe".

Thomas has missed the glory. It is the trust that matters, never the 'proof'. Still, this man who legend describes as dying an heroic martyr's death in India, is the patron saint of all those who experience doubt. Doubt is not a dead end. It can lead to an intensification of faith. It was not the other Apostles, standing reverently on either side, who acclaimed Jesus with the words "my Lord and my God". Had they realised, at last, that Jesus was truly God as well as truly man? They must

96

have been conscious of it, but perhaps not yet come to articulate so overwhelming a truth. It is doubting Thomas, the slow cautious one, who is the first to acclaim, in unforgettable words, the Godhead of Jesus, His divine Lordship.

Never mind your doubts, acclaim Him!

21.
The Ascension of Christ

6th century,
St Catherine's Monastery
Mount Sinai, Egypt.

21. THE ASCENSION OF CHRIST
6th century

21. The Ascension of Christ

6th century

The forty days after the Resurrection of Jesus must have been the most extraordinary period in Christian history. Once the Apostles had finally come to terms with the overwhelming miracle of His Presence, every day must have held out the ecstatic possibility of His appearance. We are told that, "He appeared to many". Mary Magdalene knew well that this state was only temporary, but perhaps there were those among the Apostles who persuaded themselves that He would be among them always, visible and beautiful. It was not to be. He remained on earth long enough to make it inescapably clear that He was alive – more than alive – transcendently alive. But while He was physically visible, His power was limited. He could not send the Spirit, He could not be alive in their hearts, until their knowledge of Him sprang from faith and not from sight.

This is a very early icon showing that climactic moment when Jesus said farewell in the flesh, and ascended into heaven. Western art has always been challenged by the sublimity of this image, and usually shows Mary and the Apostles, looking upwards, while there are only two feet appearing below the upper edge of the painting. For the Orthodox, this is lacking in respect. This is a damaged icon, but the image will be repeated over the centuries. Jesus is central, held in an oval mandorla of glory, the most eye catching element in the icon.

This is what we notice above all, Jesus, ascending heavenwards. Translucent angels bear him up. Soon He will disappear from sight, and only the eyes of faith will see Him, interiorly, within the heart.

Meanwhile, on earth, Mary stands astounded, lifting up her hands in praise and wonder. On either side the Apostles look upwards, bewildered, bereaved but believing. Mary does not need to look upwards. Naturally, she will miss her Son, but supernaturally she understands that this is how it must be. It is how He will draw all to Himself. He is set free from the limitations of time and place. "He has ascended to His Father". Most later icons add further elements to the story. When the Apostles got over their shock, they found "two men in white robes" rebuking them for their folly in gazing up into the heavens. Jesus will come again, they told them, but only on the last day. Meanwhile, Christians were meant to get on with life, and to live in the Spirit of Jesus, rather than hankering after His material presence. Perhaps the iconographer imagined that two of the angels, so blissfully bearing Jesus upwards, would then come down to the earth, to give sound advice to His rather hapless followers.

There are very few early icons of Jesus that survive. We are privileged to possess this image of our Blessed Lord held between heaven and earth. His garments are gilded as opposed to the earthy clothing of His mother and His Apostles. He stretches out a hand in final blessing, while His other hand holds the rolled parchment of His teaching. That teaching has yet to be written down, to comprise the Gospels and through His union with Jesus, the letters of St Paul. There might seem to be two worlds here, the eternal world of Jesus, and the temporal world of Mary and of her anxious supporters. But the whole icon is lit with an inner glory, showing us that in Jesus heaven and earth are one.

22.
The Dormition of the Virgin

12th/13th century,
Tretyakov Gallery,
Moscow.

22. THE DORMITION OF THE VIRGIN
12th/13th century

22. The Dormition of the Virgin
12th/13th century

This is the most important feast of Our Lady in the Eastern Church. It is also a great feast in the Western Church, although there it is not called the Dormition, but the Assumption; but all feasts of Our Lady are also feasts of Our Lord. It is He who gives them their sacred meaning. Here we are celebrating Mary's death. As she lies motionless, above her arises the glorious figure of her Son, gleaming and vertical. The Eastern legend has it, that when Gabriel came to Mary to tell her that her death was near, she summoned the Apostles and prepared her deathbed. This icon shows the Apostles being whirled through the air by angels, coming from all corners of the earth.

This is a remarkably peaceful icon, the Apostles crowd around either end of her bier, behind them two of the Eastern Fathers, (perhaps Theodore the Studite and John of Damascus), who have written so eloquently about this holy death. The feast of the Assumption celebrates Mary carried up to heaven by angels, body and soul. The feast of the Dormition shows Jesus Himself coming down from heaven, or rather bringing heaven with Him, to receive His Mother's soul. It is a very touching image. When He was born on earth, Mary held Him, wrapped in swaddling cloths. Now He holds her, new born into heaven, wrapped in the swaddling cloths of immortality. Jesus lifts His mother in triumph, she is His perfect disciple, the one who most truly loved and followed Him. She is His 'first fruits'.

Mary's ascent into heaven, and we notice Jesus seems to hold a physical Mary, spells out our own destiny. We too, will die temporally in the body, and become small and diminished in death, but the candle of our true life does not go out. Between the scarlet flame of the candle before the bier and the scarlet wings of the Cherubim above the head of Jesus, is a continuity. For each of us, dying in the Faith will mean the same new birth in the arms of Jesus. Mary's Dormition, Mary's Assumption, is our future as well. She had the glory of being His perfect joy. Us, He will gather in His arms, with equal love, but without the fullness of grateful delight that He found in her holiness. She rests, utterly content in His embrace. His hands are not bare, He has them covered, in the traditional mark of respect.

No one respects His creation with greater reverence than the Creator. Most of us will not rest as serenely in His arms as Mary does. In His unveiled presence, seeing Him "face to face", we will feel the immense sorrow that our sinfulness causes Him. His sorrow is on our account. Because we have not loved Him according to the fullness of whatever is our capacity, He has not been able to sanctify us as He has wished. That sanctification will take place in the purifying flames of the love that now engulfs us. We call this purgatory. There was no purgatory for the Blessed Virgin, and hence we see the exultation of her beloved Son, lifting up the radiance of her being, to display it to the world.

23.
Exultation
of the Honourable Wood
of the Cross

Early 15th century,
Suzdal Museum,
Suzdal, Russia.

23. EXULTATION
OF THE HONOURABLE WOOD OF THE CROSS
Early 15th century

23. Exultation of the Honourable Wood of the Cross

Early 15th century

T he exultation of the Holy Cross has been one of the great feasts of the Church ever since St Helena went to Jerusalem and, according to the legend, rediscovered the actual wood of the Cross on which Christ had been crucified. She was the mother of Emperor Constantine, who founded the second Rome, Constantinople, which became Byzantium. For the Orthodox Church it is almost a family feast, for it was Constantine who was the first Roman Emperor to accept the truth of Christianity. What makes this icon so striking is its understanding of means and ends. Jesus is the end, always and only the end, and we honour the Cross solely because of the use He made of it. In itself, the Cross is an instrument of torture. Taken up in love, it becomes the instrument of salvation.

The tall, elongated figure of Jesus dominates the icon. He is seen within the context of His Church, that other means to the same end, a fuller union with Jesus. On either side of Him stand His mother and St John the Baptist, which is another reference to the Church. All Orthodox Churches have as their visual centre what is called the Deisis, that is Jesus with Mary and John on either side, and beyond them, at least six Bishops or Prophets or Doctors. Only Jesus looks out at His congregation. All the holy figures, who represent us as we would wish to be, turn towards Him, to be blessed

111

and strengthened. Jesus stands upon jagged rocks which slope down to a riverbed. The rocks, however, are lit as if from within, perhaps recalling Mount Tabor. At the foot of the little mountain rises a small and almost insignificant cross. Three angels cluster around it and we can see that it stands within a river, thereby consecrating its waters. The reference is to the Pool of Siloam that we read of in the Gospel. The sick came there to be blessed, and here, on either side, we see the mass of the sick and needy. The Gospel story showed Jesus healing the sick by His presence. Now it is the spiritually sick whom He heals, and the wood of the Cross is not merely material but infused with His own redemptive grace. In becoming man, Jesus has transformed the very nature of matter. He has made everything that exists a potential means of grace. In venerating the wood of the Cross, we are specially honouring the meaning of His death. Suffering, in itself, is no more sanctifying than the dull materiality of wood. But Jesus made wood 'honourable', he used it to redeem us. The Cross is a symbol of all that causes us to suffer, in itself a dead end, through grace, blessedly redemptive.

The angels, those heavenly figures of light, clustering around the font (surely the baptismal font?) are eclipsed by the thin frailty of the Cross that rises above them, and that, in itself is only important because of the figure of Jesus. The exultation of the Cross is really the exultation of the Saviour, the redemptive Jesus, who stands within the context of His Church and draws us to Himself.

24.
Christ and St Menas

6th or 7th century,
The Louvre,
Paris.

24. CHRIST AND ST MENAS
6th or 7th century

24. Christ and St Menas

6th or 7th century

S aint Menas is one of the first and most dearly loved of the saints of Egypt. This beautiful icon comes from the Coptic Monastery of Bawit, which was once a flourishing centre of prayer in Middle Egypt. Menas, who died in 288, served in the Roman army; he became a Christian, retired to the desert to lead a life of a hermit, and was then drawn by the needs of others into a life of preaching. He is honoured as a martyr, and from the 4th century pilgrims flocked to his tomb near Alexandria. The interesting question here is whether Abbot Menas is that first, original soldier Menas, or the Abbot of the Monastery, who has taken his name. (Abbot means 'abba', father, so the title does not answer our question). Certainly this St Menas carrying an abbot's scroll and raising his hand in blessing, does not look particularly military. The point of the icon, though, is not really which St Menas he is, but of his relationship to Jesus. Jesus holds the jewelled book of His teaching in one hand, and with the other, lovingly and firmly embraces his disciple. Note how Jesus allows Menas to give the blessing: this is what it means to be his disciple. Now that the Lord is no longer visible on earth, it is only through our hands that He can bless and through our voice that He can speak.

St Menas has on his face an indescribable look of joy, humility and wonder. He does not glance aside to Jesus, it is enough to stand before us knowing that Jesus holds him, loves him, befriends him. That inward knowledge is what infuses the saint with spiritual strength and confidence.

The Coptic Church produced an art peculiar to itself. One of its distinguishing marks is the largeness of the eye. All iconographers understand the significance of the eye. Jesus, or Mary or the Saints, look at us, always face on, never in profile or aslant. The holy gaze rests on us, drawing us out of our limitations into the boundlessness of eternity where Jesus and His saints are profoundly alive. In fact, if the eyes of an icon were destroyed, the icon was reverently buried. If it could not 'see us' it had become non-functional. We must always remember that an icon can never, by its very nature, be merely a 'work of art' something decorative. It is a vital element in the actuality of Faith, and it is above all the eyes that make us aware of this.

Jesus is doing nothing here except showing His love for Menas. Menas is a saint, true enough, but it is not only because he is holy that the Lord embraces him. He embraces him because of what he himself is, love made visible. All his life, St Menas was held fast by Jesus. All our life, we are held fast by Jesus. There is no indication that St Menas ever felt that hand on his shoulder, or the warmth of Our Lord's presence at his side. He became a saint because he believed in the presence and acted by its power. How can Jesus hold us if we will not let Him? Above all, how can we learn that He is with us, if we do not stand silent, as St Menas does, in prayer? Some time for stillness is a necessity for every life. If we let Jesus hold us, when there is nothing else absorbing our attention, we may be able to remember, during the heat and fret of the day, that He is still holding us. Menas is not young. His beard is greying and his hair seems to be diminishing, as hair tends to do as we grow older. Jesus is ever young, and we feel He has been holding the Abbot for years past and will hold him for years to come. Jesus is the stability of Menas, the stability of all who receive Him, and this is a most moving depiction of what union with Our Lord means.

25.
Christ in Majesty

15th century,
National Art Museum of Ukraine,
Kiev.

25. CHRIST IN MAJESTY
15th century

25. Christ in Majesty

15th century

The theme of Christ in Majesty is the most magnificent in all iconography. We could say that this is the essential icon. Now that Jesus has ascended and is no longer physically with us, this is the icon which strives most of all to honour and reveal to us what He is. Jesus is God made Man, a mystery beyond our comprehending. This is the mystery in which we live, through faith.

This icon is traditionally written large and prominently displayed. The throne of Jesus, diaphanous and transparent in the light of eternity, is held within a pattern of two geometric shapes of scarlet. First there is a great scarlet diamond, and then, behind it, a hanging oblong with four sharp points. These eight pointed edges represent eternity, because eight is considered the mystical number of fulfilment (God created the world in six days and rested on the seventh, and on the eighth, all had been accomplished). Between the two areas of scarlet is an elongated oval of the deepest blue, the heavens. Within, swarm the Seraphim, the dark blue angels of wisdom, with their six wings and invisible bodies. Here amidst the white swirl of those glittering wings we can dimly distinguish angelic faces. Within the scarlet of the central diamond, we can see the wings of the angels of love, the Cherubim, and, third highest of the angelic hierarchy, the Thrones, wheel around the base of the throne on which Jesus sits. To complete the complexity of the symbolism, each corner of the scarlet rectangle at the rear contains an image of one of the 'living creatures' that Ezekiel saw in his Vision, and John the Evangelist saw in his Apocalypse. There are the symbols of the gospels: eagle (John), man (Matthew), ox (Luke), lion (Mark).

Angels and evangelists are only there in homage to Jesus, now ascended to His natural glory. His garments are bright with gold, yet what transfixes us is the beauty of His face - grave, thoughtful, tender. Different icons show different messages in the book that Jesus holds open. This one has a quotation from St John: "Judge not according to appearances, sons of man, but judge with right judgement". Judgement is one of the themes of Jesus' teaching: it is a function reserved to the Father. We are told: "Judge not that you may not be judged". We are asked to tread a delicate line, to see people as they are, and yet not to imagine that we can see into their hearts. The right judgement is the judgement of Jesus, and that will always be loving and true. In this icon, if one hand offers a gentle admonishment, the other offers an unambiguous blessing. However foolish the sons and daughters of men and women, we have "an advocate in the heavens". Christ in His majesty is majestic for our sakes, never for His own.

26.
Blessed Silence

Late 18th century Russian,
Temple Gallery,
London.

26. BLESSED SILENCE
Late 18th century Russian

124

26. Blessed Silence

Late 18th century Russian

There are some beautiful icons that show St John the Baptist, dressed in his traditional camel hair, but with angelic wings. A winged John makes sense, because 'angel' means messenger, and John was the messenger of the Most High sent before Jesus "to prepare His way". But it is very unusual, disconcerting, to see a winged Jesus. After all, the whole point of the Incarnation is that Jesus did not become an angel but a man, "like us in everything except sin". Yet, when we get used to it, this is a very beautiful icon. The inspiration comes from Isaiah, who spoke of "the messenger [the angel] of great counsel, who was to come". This is an icon about the essence of Jesus, His divine nature that was so indissolubly united to His humanity. He is scarlet because the Cherubim, the angels of love, are scarlet. Here we see Jesus as love itself. In a way, this is an Orthodox version of the Sacred Heart, an image known to all Catholics. But whereas the Western Church stresses how much Jesus suffered for love, the Eastern Church simply rejoices in that He is love.

Within the halo of Jesus are two four-pointed stars. Their eight points make an octave, which signifies both eternity and the completion of God's creation. Jesus wears the robes of a bishop. "We have a great high priest who has passed into the heavens, Jesus Christ, Son of God": the author of the Epistle to the Hebrews would have understood this icon. His bishop's robe is adorned with three Seraphim, the angels of wisdom. This mystical Jesus holds in one hand an eight pointed cross, and in the other a scroll, on which we can read: "come unto me all you who labour and are heavy burdened and I will give you rest".

The beautiful title, 'Blessed Silence', may have come from Isaiah's description of the Saviour as "a sheep dumb before its shearer opening not His mouth". We see this happening during the Passion. Jesus spoke when it was necessary, but when Pilate pressured Him with questions, He kept silent. There is a lovely English idiom: He held His peace.

Never in the history of humanity, has there been less silence than there is today. What with radio, television, i-pods, computers, cell phones, people can be mentally occupied from waking until they go to sleep. Yet silence is the means through which God communicates Himself. It is a human necessity to be still, to halt the busy wheels, to let God shine on us. Prayer does not mean that God will speak to us, God does not use words: Jesus is the Word. He speaks this Word that is Himself, within us, but in silence. We know His presence not so much by experience, as by the silent reverberations of that mystical closeness. Jesus, Blessed Silence, draws us with His eyes, with the implicit message of His transfigured body. He has become the red of fire to make it clear to us, without the clumsiness of words, that He is love itself.

There is a certain irony in trying to describe in words the blessedness of holy Silence. No icons can be adequately talked about. We always need to stay before them, quietly, lovingly, offering what we are to what the icon represents.

27.
The Deisis
and the Great Feasts

A Russian Immigrant,
St Vladimir Seminary,
New York.

27. THE DEISIS AND THE GREAT FEASTS
A Russian Immigrant

27. The Deisis and the Great Feasts

A Russian Immigrant

The Deisis, Jesus raising His hand in blessing over His assembled people, while His mother and St John the Baptist bow towards Him in reverence, may be the central icon of the iconostasis, but it does not stand alone. The iconostasis is the great array of icons that in the East separates the body of the Church from the sanctuary where the Holy Mysteries are celebrated. There are usually at least fourteen saints, seven on either side, bending reverently towards Our Lord: the very word 'deisis' means entreaty. As well as the saints, the iconostasis displays the great feasts of the Church, and this small icon has taken those twelve feasts and made them into a border for this central image of the Blessing Jesus. This is a condensed iconostasis, a portable replica of the imposing images that we would find in the Church.

Laid out like this, the icons make it clear that the whole Christian faith is totally dependent on Jesus. These twelve mysteries are all depictions of Jesus at work. He is not visible in the very first icon, one might think, when Gabriel announces to the Virgin that she has been chosen to be God's mother. Yet He is visible in minute, almost vestigial, form from above the ray of light which carries towards Mary's womb the tiny form of the unborn Jesus. Jesus may be almost unseen but this is genuinely an image of the iconic Jesus: He is its meaning.

He is also not visible in the second to last icon, the descent of the Holy Spirit. We see the Apostles waiting in the upper room, we see the symbol of the Church ready to receive the gift of God, we see the flames of fire. But the Spirit that is given, with such transforming power, is what St Paul rightly describes as, "the Spirit of Jesus". This Holy Spirit has come down upon the Church, to be 'with it always', keeping it true to its Saviour. In all the other ten icons Jesus is central, even in the one icon that is non scriptural, the very last, where He comes to receive His mother's soul on her deathbed. Placing the icons of Jesus' life around the central image emphasises that there is no Church, no Faith except for Jesus. He is our great mediator, salvation is only through Him, "no one can come to the Father except through Me".

When Jesus founded His Church 'upon the rock of Peter', all was very simple. He had lived His life to the full, and His Apostles were well aware of the sacred significance of all that He had said and done. This icon shows us the highlights, but they take their meaning from our knowledge of their context. Yet, inevitably, in the course of time the Church has become complicated. Theologians over the centuries have delved deep into the scriptures so as to formulate Christian dogma with exactitude. The millions throughout the world who are privileged to believe in Jesus have had to be organised into parishes and dioceses, with priests and bishops and archbishops and cardinals and the Pope. It can all seem top heavy. We can hear people saying that they believe in Jesus but not in the 'church'. They are wrong. It is the Church that gives us Jesus. It may be only a means to the end that is Christ, but it is a means that we need. Throughout the centuries, the

Church has preserved the Faith, has made it possible for the contemporary Christian to contemplate icons such as this, and to understand what they mean. The Church is not just its clerics, though they are its public face. The Church is the body of the faithful, held in their faith by the ministry of the countless priests and bishops who have given their lives to help us understand the meaning of Jesus.

28.
The Last Judgement

12th century,
St Catherine's Monastery,
Mount Sinai, Egypt.

28. THE LAST JUDGEMENT
12th century

28. The Last Judgement

12th century

The Catechism tells us that the Four Last Things are death, judgement, hell and heaven. Death is intensely personal, the moment when each of us individually, alone, encounters the love of God. It is difficult to portray in an icon, but judgement, hell and heaven have always drawn the attention of iconographers, even though the subject is profoundly complex.

In this icon, central, enclosed in a golden mandorla, sits our Judge, Jesus Himself. Angels sing in exultation behind Him, the Virgin Mary and St John the Baptist incline in reverence on either side, and we see the twelve Apostles, seated, as He promised, on twelve thrones "to judge the tribes of Israel". They are holding open books in which are written all the words and actions of humanity. In the second tier of the icon, an angel is rolling up the sky like a scroll, as was prophesied by St John in the Apocalypse. Time has ended, place is no more, from now on there is only the eternity of heaven and hell. From the very throne of Jesus there flows a river of fire which broadens out in the third tier into a lake. Beside that lake, in a terrifying blackness, rears up the hideous animal shape of the devil. Angels are shepherding towards that horror two pathetic people.

Our faith demands that we believe in hell, and so does our common sense. If we have free will, we must have the ability to say no. Yet faith does not demand that we believe that there is anybody actually in hell. This miserable pair shrink from the hellish beast, and they are still engulfed in that great lake of fire, that purifying love, that streams from Jesus. The icon seems indubitably to suggest that in the purification of divine love, even the most hardened sinner will repent and step back from a final rejection. In the centre of the icon, on a line with the lake of fire, is what is called 'the throne prepared for judgement'. Judgement has not yet taken place, (hence the hope for every sinner), but it is imminent. Soon, Jesus will move down to the throne, which is adorned with the symbols of His Passion. Very small at its feet – we almost need a magnifying glass – are Adam and Eve. Behind them are the tiers of the Old Testament patriarchs and prophets, as well as Christian saints. These seem to have organised themselves into their ecclesiastical groups: martyrs, virgins and bishops. Below them, in the last double tier, to the left, is paradise. Mary is the Queen and with her are Abraham and Lazarus, both attested in the scriptures as having entered into heaven. It is a paradise garden, with a fiery cherub of love to guard its gates. Before the gates stands the celestial doorkeeper, St Peter, supported by three Fathers of the Church. Meanwhile, to the right, angels help men and beasts to arise from death and to enter the glory of heaven.

Amidst all these small and attentive figures waiting eagerly, perhaps fearfully, to receive their judgement, our attention is focused on Our Lord. Our judge is the one who gave His life for us, who "loved us to the end". When He takes His seat upon 'the throne prepared for judgement', we will see Him surrounded by images that recall His passion, and we will remember how much He loves us, and be comforted.

29.
At Your Right Hand
Stands The Queen

c. 1380, Serbian working in Novgorod,
Cathedral of the Dormition,
Kremlin, Moscow.

29. AT YOUR RIGHT HAND STANDS THE QUEEN
A Serbian working in Novgorod

29. At Your Right Hand Stands The Queen

A Serbian working in Novgorod

This golden image has several layers of meaning. On one level, it is an icon of Christ, the King of Kings. He is dressed in the robes of a Russian Czar, and His mother is dressed as a Queen. The reference is to Psalm 45: "At your right hand stands the Queen in gold of Ophir". These words hark back to the Queen of Sheba who came to visit Solomon anxious to learn from his wisdom: because Solomon's gold came 'from Ophir'. But Mary as Queen represents far more than the Queen of Sheba, and as we know from the gospels, when we look at Jesus, we are aware "there is greater than Solomon here". This image of Kingly Jesus and Queenly Mary celebrate the marriage of Christ as Bridegroom and Mary as the Church, the Bride. The significance of St John the Baptist, who is so honoured in the Orthodox deisis, standing to one side of Jesus as does Mary on the other, is that he represents 'the bridegroom's friend'. (In modern language, we would call him the best man.) The bridegroom was always accompanied by this special friend, and John holds in his hand a scroll on which is written: "he who has the bride is the bridegroom; the friend of the bridegroom who stands and hears him, rejoices greatly". This quotation comes from the Gospel of St John, and it is a poetic summary of the vital function of the Baptist. He understood that Jesus had come to preach the Kingdom and that as King He would take as bride, His Church. This Church He would always, like a husband, (St Paul is very eloquent on this), protect and cherish with love. Of course, the beautiful Virgin, in her golden attire, is the ideal Church. Yet Jesus has married 'the real Church', with all its weaknesses and failure to understand. We see this even in the embryonic church of Peter and the Apostles. Whatever their blunders and desertions and failures, His love remained unfaltering.

But this is also an icon of Christ the High Priest. Sometimes this image bears the words: "you are a priest forever, according to the order of Melchizedek". We do not need the actual words because Christ is not only dressed as a King, but as a priest. When He was born, the Magi offered gifts of gold, frankincense and myrrh. He was too small to understand it then, but the gold was in honour of His Kingship, and the frankincense in honour of His priesthood. As would become sorrowfully clear, myrrh had been brought, in advance, for His burial. This is not a myrrh icon, it is all gold and frankincense, glorying in the sacred power of Our Saviour. Western art is drawn to the suffering Jesus and to move us to contrition. Eastern art, where the image is of incalculably deeper significance, prefers rather to contemplate Jesus in His glory.

30.
Christ the True Vine

Late 16th century,
Byzantine Museum,
Athens, Greece.

30. CHRIST THE TRUE VINE
Late 16th century

30. Christ the True Vine

Late 16th century

At the Last Supper, "knowing that His hour had come", Jesus opened His heart to His Apostles. One can doubt how much they understood, but they remembered, and in the years ahead, they must have meditated again and again on these words so translucent with His Spirit. The great gift at that Supper was to be the gift of the Holy Eucharist. That is a gift of such mystical fullness that no human mind can ever plumb its depths. In the Mass, Jesus gives Himself, all that He is, taking us with Him to the Father. We can never say a total 'yes'. St Paul says of Jesus: "yes was always in Him. He is our great Amen to the Father". United to Jesus in the Eucharist, we can utter, through His Spirit, that total 'yes' that is beyond our unaided power.

But how was Jesus to explain to His poor, fumbling Apostles, so deep a mystery? They knew Him as Man, and believed, more or less truthfully, that they loved Him. After His death though, they would know Him from within, sacramentally, in the Eucharist. The image Jesus uses, in a poetic attempt to help their understanding, is that of the vine, a plant familiar to them all. He tells them: "I am the true Vine, and My Father is the Vine dresser. Every branch of Mine that bears no fruit, He takes away, and every branch that does bear fruit He prunes so that it bears more fruit". He stresses this metaphor, "I am the Vine and you are the branches". We contemplate these words with wonder. The vine and its branches are one, there is no distinction. Jesus is telling us that His Eucharistic gift of Himself so unites us to Him that we too are part of 'the true vine'. It is only if we 'bear no fruit', if we will not receive the sap of love that gives life to the vine, that the Father will cut us away. He warns us, of course, that when we receive this Holy Sap, and 'bear fruit', the Heavenly Vine dresser is not complacent. He will 'prune' us always out of love, so that we will bear 'more fruit'.

Often this mystical theme was embroidered on liturgical vestments. Here is a beautiful example with Jesus dominating His vine, holding an open gospel on His knees so as to leave both arms free for a wide gesture of blessing. It could even be seen as a gesture of prayerful jubilation, Jesus rejoicing in the sturdiness of His Church. There are twelve shoots, rich with leaf and grape, and on the branches sit the Apostles. Closest to Jesus are St Peter and St Paul. Prolonged contemplation of the icon will make it possible to identify each Apostle. They have their initials near their halos and also hold their traditional attributes. (St John, for example, holds a chalice). This is the secret truth of the Church, that it is indeed a holy vine springing from the presence of the Eternal Jesus. This is not the Church which we see, the bedraggled and all too human church, slowly learning to enter into 'the mind of Christ'. Humanly, this church does not seem intimately united with Jesus, as is the branch with the tree. But that is only humanly speaking, that is what 'seems'. In the light of eternity, this is a true icon summoning us to enter into its Holy Truth.

31.
Praise The Lord

16th/17th century Russian,
National Museum,
Stockholm.

31. PRAISE THE LORD
16th/17th century Russian

31. Praise The Lord
16th/17th century Russian

We remember the distress of Jesus when He healed ten lepers, and only one, the Samaritan at that, returned to give thanks. He was not distressed for His own sake. Doing good was natural to Jesus, part of His very being. No, He was distressed for the sake of the healed lepers because without gratitude, we cannot become fully human. As scripture tells us, we have nothing "that we have not received". The man or woman who is fully alive, is aware of their existential truth. There is an infinitude that they have received, and it is God who has given it. It has been wisely said, that the essential words are, 'thank you'.

To praise God is to understand what we are, what we can be, and what we need. This icon makes visible the happiness of living in that holy praise. Jesus in Himself, of course, is the Great Incarnate Praise of God. Here, in the vast concentric circles of the heavens, He orchestrates the praise of creation, which ascends to the Father through Him. It is Jesus who knows the Father, it is through Jesus that we too know that unutterable Mystery. Not in the heavens, as is Jesus, but on the solid ground of our earth, throng the believers, whose faith is in Jesus. There are priests there and kings, men and women, clerics and lay folk, all united in a great hymn of gratitude. Above them, in the heavens with Jesus, though not in the great multicoloured sphere that encompasses Him, are the saints. They have become saints precisely because they understood the need to 'praise the Lord'. Prominent among them, nearest to Jesus as she always will be, is Our Blessed Lady. We remember her great song of gratitude to God began with the words, "My soul glorifies the Lord and my spirit rejoices in God my Saviour". This is an icon of rejoicing as Mary says. The whole world is filled 'with the glory of the Lord', and our awareness of it is a profound joy.

Yet, it is not only we who are privileged to share a human nature with Jesus, who are called upon to enter into this joyful praise. Most touchingly, the icon summons the entire world. There are trees waving blissfully in the centre of the icon. (There is a line in the psalms which reads, "all the trees of the forest shout for joy"). Immediately beneath the ecstatic trees, is the animal dearest to the scriptures, the lamb. This is the small creature that will receive the honour of being a symbol of Jesus Himself: He was "the Lamb of God". But the icon painter lets loose his imagination picturing horses and snakes and boars and various other rather indeterminate animals. They may not have minds to know the Lord or wills to choose to follow Him, but in their innocence, they praise Him by existing. To be created, in any form, is to be held in the Creator's Hand. Knowingly or unknowingly, all creation is summoned by Jesus to join Him in an absolute of blessed praise.

32.
The Non-Sleeping Eye

Early 16th century Russian,
Icon Museum,
Recklinghausen, Germany.

32. THE NON-SLEEPING EYE
Early 16th century Russian

32. The Non-Sleeping Eye

Early 16th century Russian

The 'Eye of God' has been an image that has struck fear into many a sinful heart. "Thou, God, seeth me". Yet, the last emotion that this icon would inspire is that of fear. The 'non-sleeping eye', that unwavering attention that God pays to each of His creatures, is rather an occasion for comfort and gratitude. The icon shows Christ Emmanuel, at rest in a garden, surrounded by flowering trees and trustful birds. 'Emmanuel' means 'God is with us', another version of His unsleeping Eye. Christ Emmanuel is always shown young and beautiful. To some degree, this is the young Jesus, but in a deeper sense, this is the Eternal Jesus: Christ yesterday, today and for ever. He is eternally youthful, fresh, free of the stresses that will burden the earthly Jesus and bring Him to His death.

Yet, however idyllic the setting for this sleeping Jesus may seem, there is a subtext. The angel who leans over Him with such solicitude is holding a cross, and in many versions of this icon, there is beneath the sleeping Jesus, the open mouth of a sepulchre. Here, at this moment, He is free, like the soaring birds: it will not last. The half circle at the edge of the upper part of the icon is a symbol of the presence of God. From that holy circle come protecting rays, shielding the sleeping Christ. His mother, bending over Him with loving care, and the angel reverently holding out the cross, form a protective shield, emphasised by the trees. The inspiration for the icon comes from the psalms: "He who watches Israel slumbers not nor sleeps". The wakeful slumber of Jesus Emmanuel is for our sake, just as His death will be for our sake, and this is equally true for every action and word of His life. 'God with us' is also 'God for us'. God watches us, without respite, only and always so as to care for us. That is why this young Jesus is also an ever young Jesus, a trans-historical figure. The actual human Jesus grew weary and slept as we all do, but as God, our Eternal Lover, He is ever wakeful, anxious to forestall our needs, eager to be with us in our difficulties.

That "Thou God seeth me", should be our great joy. We are never left alone in our human inadequacy, we are never un-loved.

This icon, so tenderly revealing the vigilant love of our Em-manuel Christ, is an exquisite example of Russian icons at their most sensitive and delicate. It is almost impossible to put into words the beauty and the loving sweetness of this scene. It reminds us, (see the rocks along the lower edge of the icon), that the paradise garden is only temporary in this world. Soon Jesus must stand erect, receive the cross, and de-scend into the harshness of His future. But the paradise gar-den, where He watches out for us, is eternal in the heavens, and for us who believe in Him, who look at Him while He looks at us, that is the Reality. Prayer is letting God look at us, His gaze drawing our gaze. It is Jesus who prays: St Paul describes it as uttering within us "sighs too deep for words". We need no words. We need only to be still and let the Non-Sleeping Eye draw us into the holiness of the Father.

33.
Christ Pantokrator

6th century,
St Catherine's Monastery,
Mount Sinai, Egypt.

33. CHRIST PANTOKRATOR
6th century

33. Christ Pantokrator

6th century

From the 8th century until half way through the 9th century, the Byzantine Empire set about destroying all its icons. Wherever holy images existed, they were burnt, thrown into rivers, hacked to pieces, whitewashed if on walls, scribbled over if in books. From this iconoclastic fury hardly anything has survived. There are eight icons of the Virgin Mary, mostly kept safe in Rome where the Byzantine Emperor had no power, and for the rest there is only a pathetic and damaged number of ancient icons in the remote desert monastery of St Catherine. Supreme among these pre-iconoclastic images, is this magnificent icon of Christ the Ruler of All, the Pantokrator.

The icon painter never invented, never inaugurated. The whole point of the icon was that it was true, this was a real image. The Mandylion, said to have been miraculously imprinted on a cloth, set the standard for the icon of Jesus. He is dark haired, brown eyed, He has a slight beard, a strong and powerful neck, and an air of majesty. This exceptionally early icon captures with grace and beauty what the early Christians saw as the essence of Our Saviour. In those far off centuries, the truth of the Faith was still imperilled. There were Christians who believed that there was only a Divine Jesus, and the human Jesus was just a pretence. They could not face the reality of His physical presence. There were equally

Christians that denied His full divinity, and saw Jesus as the greatest of the prophets but not as the Son of God. This icon expresses that holy union of the two natures, divine and human. It was because Jesus was human, that there could be icons made of Him. In worshipping that humanity, we are drawn into that divinity which we cannot see, but in which we believe. In the 6th century there was a passionate need to establish the reality of the God-Man of Christ the Pantokrator, the All Powerful.

Against a dimly glimpsed background of the real world – we can see mountains, fields, buildings, trees – Jesus stands erect. His great halo has been gilded, blotting out the sky with its brightness. In one hand He holds the book of the Gospels, glittering with gold and jewels and marked with a cross. This is the only reference in the icon to His sufferings. His other hand is raised in the traditional blessing, in which the fingers form the initials, in Greek, of His name: IC XC.

There has never been a more powerful image of the beauty and holiness of Our Lord. We are held by the searching look in His eyes and comforted by the grace of His countenance and of His blessing.

34.
Christ the Saviour

c. 1420, Andrei Rublev,
Tretykov Gallery,
Moscow.

34. CHRIST THE SAVIOUR
Andrei Rublev

34. Christ the Saviour

Andrei Rublev

About nine hundred years later than the first image of the Saviour in His Majestic Reality, the image now preserved in St Catherine's Monastery at Mount Sinai, there was another and equally beautiful masterpiece, created in 15th century Russia. The image is so striking that there is universal agreement, though there is no definite proof, that it could only have been painted by the great Andrei Rublev. All iconographers regard their task as a sacred vocation. It is a means of prayer, of surrendering to God so that He can manifest through the artist the holiness of His truth. Though icon painters aspire to this, there is perhaps only one of whom we can be certain that his work sanctified him. Andrei Rublev has been officially canonised, though all who know his work do not need this seal of officialdom.

His Jesus, painted at a time when the teachings of the Church were fully stabilised, is remarkable less for its power, though it is powerful indeed, than for its gentleness. Christ the Great Judge appears before us as a figure of infinite tenderness and compassion. He is visibly possessed by the Holy Spirit. Rublev suggests that Jesus is turning towards us, emphasising His awareness of our need and His loving eagerness to meet it. It is unmistakably the same Jesus of the 6th century, yet seen by a medieval artist faithful to the original image but transfusing this lovely face with his own prayerful tenderness.

The icon is in a battered condition. At some time in Russian history it had been used as part of a floor in a wood shed. It was discovered only by sheer accident in 1918. Somehow the damage, the loss of paint, the scratches, makes the image an even more poignant expression of the Saviour's mercy: He too knows what it means to suffer. The Eastern Father of the Church, John of Damascus, has written: "I saw the human face of God, and my soul was saved". The intimacy with which this damaged face looks out on us, is a moving reminder of what Jesus is. He is one who has come to unite us to Himself, and His merciful love would overcome all difficulties.

The Blessing
of Christ Our Saviour

35. CHRIST THE SAVIOUR
Aidan Hart

35. Christ the Saviour

Aidan Hart

There must be thousands of icons that show the face of Christ: He is after all the centre of our Faith, it is Jesus who gives meaning to our lives. I have never seen one more beautiful than this 21st century icon by the well-known British iconographer, Brother Aidan Hart. It is a completely traditional icon, not one with a costly gold background, but with the equally conventional pink, with the blue cross of a notional halo. This is an icon to pray before, so that we can respond to the prayer with which it has been painted. It needs few words, we can all see what it is, and what it offers of union with the Lord it venerates. It sometimes strikes me that the frame can hardly contain the living reality of this Saviour. There is no room for His halo and even the traditional alpha and omega, found in so many icons, have to squeeze themselves out of the icon and onto the frame. Jesus transcends all our loving attempts to depict Him.

36. CHRIST THE SAVIOUR
Stephane Rene

36. Christ the Saviour

Stephane Rene

Stephane Rene, like Aidan Hart, is renowned world-wide. Here are exactly the same details that we find in the 6th century. Jesus holds the book of the Bible, and lifts His hand in blessing. The fingers here do not spell out the initials of His name, these are inscribed in the gold background. What distinguishes this beautiful icon is its sense of order and dignity. Here is an image remote from the chaos of our world. "Come to me all you who labour and are heavy burdened and I will give you rest". Here is that rest made visible, a rest available to all who will stay silent before the holy icon.

37. CHRIST THE LORD
Sr Veronica Comer ODC

37. Christ the Lord

Sr Veronica Comer ODC

This striking image of the Lord seems very clearly the fruit of prayer. It was painted – or, as the iconographers prefer, written - by a contemplative nun. Jesus seems to be looking into the distance, absorbed by the presence of His Father. We pass through the physicality of His presence into that divine stillness which is so central to Him. Once again, the confines of the frame only emphasise the greatness of Jesus. His halo extends beyond what we can see. Like all true icons, it draws us into the mystery of Christ, that infinite source of Christian contemplation.

38. CHRIST THE LORD
20th century Russian

38. Christ the Lord

20th century Russian

This is a very small and anonymous icon set deep into a little block of wood. Whoever painted it had a good sense of the ancient tradition, since all the elements are here. But he cannot help giving this Jesus a 20th century appearance. It is a beautiful face, alight with dignity and grace, and it may well speak more directly to the contemporary heart than the great masterpieces of early Christianity. Yet we feel that his conscious intention was only to follow these traditions, to be faithful, and to show us the true Face of Christ.

39. CHRIST BLESSING
19th century Russian

39. Christ Blessing
19th century Russian

This is a very powerful image of Jesus in His majesty. The splendour and intricacy of the gold background makes us keenly aware of His sunburned complexion and the dark radiance of His eyes. He holds very high the white pages of His Gospel book, which again emphasises that our Jesus was a Palestinian Jew. Printed clearly on these open pages are words from Scripture "Come unto me and I will give you rest."

The writing at the base of the frame reads: "The magical (mystical) picture of the Saviour in Moskvoretskiy Chapel in Moscow."

Jesus may be dark of face, but He seems to be lit with an inner glow. The more we pray before this icon, the more it opens up to us and draws us into the Godhead.

40. CHRIST BLESSING
19th century Russian

40. Christ Blessing

19th century Russian

This is not an outstanding icon but the very sense of frailty that seems to emanate from it is touching. Here we have indeed the 'gentle Jesus' with whom we are always at home and whose slender hand is always raised in blessing. The large Gospel book is open at the pages that read: "Come unto me and I will give you rest."

For centuries, every Orthodox Christian carried with them, or kept close at hand, an icon such as this one. It is probably faded because of the years it has been exposed to sunlight, kept in a pocket, put to spiritual use. An icon does not have to be a great work of art to be fully functional. Any icon can draw us into the presence of Jesus.

41. CHRIST THE ALMIGHTY
19th/20th century Greek

41. Christ the Almighty

19th/20th century Greek

This is an icon of Christ blessing with one hand, as is traditional, but with the other holding, not the book of His Gospel, but the round disc of the world. It is His world, it is safe within His grasp. Jesus died to save that world, and perhaps the gleaming blue-white of the sphere is a suggestion of the innocence that closeness to Him will bring.

Greek Orthodox monasteries receive countless pilgrims from all over the Orthodox world. When the Russian Church was persecuted, it was the other branches of the Orthodox Faith that kept alive the significance of the icon. This is in no sense 'a special icon'. It is representative of the icons that the monks painted within the monastery, to give or sell to the pilgrims who wanted to take back a memorial of their visit. We do not know from which monastery this particular icon came, but it was found in the West, and so we can be practically certain that some devoted pilgrim carried it away with him or her. It would have been frequently kissed, revered, kept in some small home. It seems to carry with it all that history of devotion.

42. CHRIST THE ALMIGHTY
20th century

42. Christ the Almighty
20th century

This was an inexpensive icon displayed in a shop alongside larger and smaller versions of the same image. We could call it, I suppose, a 'commercial icon'. It has not been painted in traditional iconographic fashion, but half-moulded out of some metallic substance. Why I include it as an instance of the Iconic Jesus is because I find so touching the attempt to make glorious an image that we could easily pass by as vulgar. Great icons had often a background of true gold, many were richly adorned with silver, they were studded with jewels. The devout lavished their wealth on the material image, in an attempt to do homage to the immaterial Godhead. I see here a brave attempt to pay this homage. There are bright jewels at every corner, even though they are coloured glass. The halo, made from a cheap metal, is embossed, and again there are glass flowers to provide as much beauty as is possible. The purist will shrink. Yet this truly is an icon. There are the syllables of Our Lord's Name IC XC, there are Alpha and Omega, there is the blessing hand, and there is the Gospel book which contains a selection of Greek symbols and words which celebrate the redemption of all humanity in Christ.

We go through the icon to the Christ it represents, whatever the poverty of the representation.

Further reading

I looked through very many collections of icons
to choose the ones in this book, but there are
two books that I feel everyone would profit
by reading.

The first is a deeply contemplative book:
Icon: Divine Beauty, by Richard Temple, 2004,
Saqi Books. (Sir Richard has a unique love
and understanding of the icon).

Far less contemplative but very useful
(and inexpensive) is: *Icons and Saints
of the Eastern Orthodox Church,* 2004,
Getty Publications.

Acknowledgements and Permissions

Every effort has been made to acknowledge the owner of the copyright material contained in this book. The Publisher would be pleased to hear from any copyright owner who has been omitted or incorrectly acknowledged.

1. *The Icon of the Virgin and Child*
   6th or 7th century
   © Temple Gallery, London

2. *The Finding in the Temple*
   Novgorod
   Late 15th century
   © Temple Gallery, London

3. *Mid Pentecost*
   Novgorod
   Early 16th century
   The Menil Collection, Houston
   Paul Hester

4. *The Baptism of Christ*
   Mid 16th century Galychyna.
   Tempera, silvering on gesso-grounded
   two piece lime wood panel,
   canvas on the joint
   of panels stamping, 90x61x2
   © National Art Museum of Ukraine

5. *The Miracle of Cana*
   1315-1321
   © Monastery of Chora,
   Kariyecami, Istanbul, Turkey

6. *The Transfiguration*
   Theophanes the Greek
   1403
   © Tretyakov Gallery, Moscow

7. *Prayer of Petition*
   Greek or Cretan
   17th century
   © Temple Gallery, London

8. *The Parable of the Widow's Mite*
   Dionysius and his sons
   1500-1502
   © Museum of Dionysius's Frescoes, Ferapontov

9. *Christ at the Well*
   Aidan Hart
   20th century

10. *The Raising of Lazarus*
    Byzantine
    Benaki Museum, Athens
    © 2011. Photo SCALA, Florence

11. *Entrance into Jerusalem*
    Romanian
    18th century
    © Temple Gallery, London

12. *Jesus Washes the Feet of the Disciples*
    13th century
    © St Catherine's Monastery
    at Mount Sinai

13. *Communion of the Apostles*
    Private collection
    Early 17th century
    © Temple Gallery, London

30. *Christ the True Vine*
Second half of the 16th century
© Byzantine Museum,
Athens, Greece

31. *Praise The Lord*
Late 16th to early 17th century
© Moscow, National Museum,
Stockholm

32. *The Non-Sleeping Eye*
Russian
Beginning of the 16th century
© Icon Museum, Recklinghausen,
Germany

33. *Christ Pantokrator*
6th century
© St Catherine's Monastery
at Mount Sinai

34. *Christ the Saviour*
Andrei Rublev
c. 1420
© Tretyakov Gallery, Moscow

35. *Christ the Saviour*
Aidan Hart
2007
Private Collection

36. *Christ the Saviour*
Stephane Rene
2008
Private Collection

37. *Christ the Lord*
Sr Veronica Comer, ODC
2008
Private Collection

38. *Christ the Lord*
Russian
20th century
Private Collection

39. *Christ Blessing*
Russian
19th century
Private Collection

40. *Christ Blessing*
Russian
19th century
Private Collection

41. *Christ the Almighty*
Greek
Late 19th or early 20th century
Private Collection

42. *Christ the Almighty*
20th century